REACHING
PROFESSIONALS IN METROPOLISES

Practical Strategies for the 21st Century Church

DR. RALPH BAEZA

Xulon
PRESS

Copyright © 2014 by Dr. Ralph Baeza

Reaching Professionals in Metropolises
Practical Strategies for the 21st Century Church
by Dr. Ralph Baeza

Printed in the United States of America

ISBN 9781498411394

All rights reserved solely by the author. The author guarantees all contents are original and do not infringe upon the legal rights of any other person or work. No part of this book may be reproduced in any form without the permission of the author. The views expressed in this book are not necessarily those of the publisher.

Scripture quotations taken from the New American Standard Bible (NASB). Copyright © 1960, 1962, 1963, 1968, 1971, 1972, 1973, 1975, 1977, 1995 by The Lockman Foundation. Used by permission. All rights reserved.

www.xulonpress.com

Dedication

To my God, Who created me for His special and specific purpose, to be His son and servant in order to give Him all glory and honor in my life, which is His, now and forever.

To my beloved wife and lifetime companion, Alice, our three daughters, Mary Elizabeth, Georgette Josephine, and Natalie Denise and my sons-in-law, Leodanny, Benjamin, and Daniel, and my granddaughter Ava all of whom are precious gifts from God for me to treasure, love, appreciate, value, cherish, prize, serve, and give them my life as an example of commitment to pursue the presence, knowledge, and service of my Lord and Savior Jesus Christ.

To my Spaniard Heritage given by God, who allowed me to be born in Madrid, Spain, where both of my parents met during their days as students at the "Universidad Complutense de Madrid" in the 1950's. Furthermore, I am grateful for my Andalucian ethnic and cultural background from the provinces of Malaga and Jaen in Spain, where my mother, Maria Isabel Baeza, grandparents, Salvador Baeza and Juana Aguilar, and my uncles, Gumersindo Aguilar, Alonso Aguilar, Consuelo Aguilar, Andres Aguilar, and Sebastian Aguilar were all born. They and the culture of Spain taught me values of honor, integrity, and morality which have helped me to pursue a life in the service of my Lord and Savior Jesus Christ.

To all who had or have lived, preached, taught, and written for my Lord and Savior Jesus Christ, fulfilling His Great Commission to live righteous and godly lives and to make disciples of all nations. Some of these influential people, whose example have been an inspiration in my life pilgrimage on Earth, are the Apostle Paul, Rodrigo

Diaz de Vivar (The Cid), Brother Lawrence, David Livingston, Hudson Taylor, Charles Spurgeon, Dwight L. Moody, Oswald Chambers, Jerry Falwell, Robert Beatty, Gary Cohen, Elmer Towns, John MacArthur, James Dobson, Charles Swindoll, David Jeremiah, James McDonald, Norman Geisler, Luis Palau, Harold Wilmington, Ravi Zacharias, and many others who were given the privilege by God to affect many generations of believers in Christendom.

Table of Contents

Acknowledgments . . . . **vii**
Preface . . . . **ix**
Introduction: The Mission Is Still the Same . . . . **xi**

Chapter 1: The Professional Mission Field **15**
Chapter 2: Understanding the Professional Environment **22**
Chapter 3: Past and Current Trends in Reaching Professionals . . . **32**
Chapter 4: Biblical Principles to Outreach Professionals **46**
**Chapter 5: Practical Implications to Outreach Professionals in North
           America Metropolises and Beyond** **65**
Conclusions: Reaching Professionals **89**

Appendices
APPENDIX A: Contemporary Ministry Methods 93
APPENDIX B: Professional Gatherings Program Sample 110
APPENDIX C: Professional Gatherings Topics for Evangelism
             Sample 112
APPENDIX D: Professional Gatherings Topics for Discipleship
             Sample 113
APPENDIX E: Practical Experiences from the Lives of
             Professionals 115
APPENDIX F: A Call to Simplicity by Professionals 119
APPENDIX G: A Practical Implementation of Reaching and
             Equipping Professionals in a Local Church 122
APPENDIX H: Some Website Resources 126
APPENDIX I: A Prayer for the Professionals Ministry 127

Bibliography **129**
Glossary **137**
About the Author **141**
Endnotes **143**

Acknowledgements

The work of God is a team-led effort in which He gives believers abilities and resources to carry out the call of the ministry. He allowed many believers to contribute to this work; therefore, eternal gratitude is given to God and the following brethren in our Lord and Savior Jesus Christ who were part of the thesis work which was the foundation for this book.

I thank God for being the reason for my existence and all the people He sent to be a support and inspiration of this believer's life in order for this work to be a reality for His glory and honor.

I thank Dr. Falwell and Dr. Towns for following their call by God to build Liberty University and Liberty Baptist Theological Seminary; Dr. Schmitt and Dr. Rick Rasberry, for all their support and inspiration in my Doctor of Ministry thesis research which is this work foundation; all my professors in the Doctor of Ministry program at Liberty Baptist Theological Seminary: Dr. Towns, Dr. Schmitt, Dr. Davidson, Dr. Rice, and Dr. Hawkins for their dedication to teach me biblical truths and their practical implications in my personal life and ministry, and Dr. Miller for taking his valuable time to give me research guidelines.

I thank all my brethren in the Lord and Savior Jesus Christ who participated in the surveys for taking the time to provide me with their feedback.

I thank all my professors in the Master of Divinity program at Liberty Baptist Theological Seminary: Dr. Towns, Dr. Diemer, Dr. Giese, Dr. Hawkins, and others who taught me Bible-based knowledge in order to help me understand about Church ministries in this postmodern world.

I thank all my professors in the Master of Arts (Religion) program at Trinity Evangelical Divinity School (TEDS): Dr. Beatty, Dr. Cohen, Dr. Aquila, Dr. Carballosa, and Dr. Roy for the wonderful biblically based learning experience which started with a course in New Testament Backgrounds with Dr. Cohen in the Winter of 1986 at Miami Christian College and ended with an Integrative Paper course with Dr. Beatty in the Spring of 2006.

I thank Dr. Kefauver and the Xulon publishing team for the outstanding effort and commitment to make this book a reality

I thank my wife Alice Baeza for her love and support during this once in eternity life pilgrimage on Earth, in the pursuit of the call of God for our lives. I thank my daughters, Mary Garcia, Georgette Baeza Kores, and Natalie Baeza Sloan who spent countless hours in writing and editing this work, and their continuous and unconditional love and support. I thank my sons-in-law, Leodanny, Benjamin and Daniel, who gave emotional support, and for their contribution to help this book become a reality.

I am looking forward to the day we all gather in heaven to worship and thank God to be His servants and a part of His eternal purpose by our participation in this work.

Preface

This book is the result of my three-decade life pilgrimage as a Christian professional in an urban metropolis in North America. I was born in Madrid, Spain, and immigrated to Honduras in 1974 after losing my mother and grandparents. Shortly after arriving in Honduras, I was introduced to the gospel of the Lord Jesus Christ by missionaries from Florida Bible College during a worship service held Good Friday, 1975, at a Youth Camp.

Accepting Jesus Christ ignited a passion within me to devote a lifetime to serving God's purpose, but application to attend Florida Bible College in 1977 was denied due to visa issues. Remaining in Honduras, I met and married a Roman Catholic Palestinian while attending the National University of Honduras. I graduated with a Bachelor of Science in Electrical Engineering, a Bachelor of Science in Industrial Engineering, and a Master of Business Administration. I pursued a career in the consulting engineering field, first in Honduras and then in the United States after immigrating once more in 1986.

Furthermore, I completed seminary training at Trinity Evangelical Divinity School, where I graduated with a Master of Arts in Religion degree, and Liberty Baptist Theological Seminary, where I graduated with a Master of Divinity and a Doctor of Ministry degrees. I have been working as a professional consulting engineer, building a family, participating in several church ministries, and pursuing a relationship with God. The combination of all these experiences has given me firsthand knowledge of the unique challenges faced by professionals who seek a closer and deeper relationship with Christ.

Introduction
The Mission Is Still the Same

And Jesus came up and spoke to them, saying, "All authority has been given to Me in heaven and on earth. [19] Go therefore and make disciples of all the nations, baptizing them in the name of the Father and the Son and the Holy Spirit, [20] teaching them to observe all that I commanded you; and lo, I am with you always, even to the end of the age." (Matthew 28:18-20)

"The MISSION is still the same, proclaim and live the truth in Jesus name..."[1] These lyrics by Christian music author and singer Steve Green speak the foundation of the mission for this work. The mission is to create Bible-based methods which can be used by Christian leaders and professionals to reach the professional population. The methods are in accordance with the principles found in Matthew 28:18-20 to evangelize and disciple the people of the world.

> John Piper writes, "This passage is often called the 'Great Commission.' The first thing to make clear about it is still binding on a modern church. It was given not only to the apostles for their ministry but also the Church for its ministry as long as this age lasts."[2]

The American Church in Crisis by David Olson gives statistics which show that the modern day church is operating in a "last century mindset." It also makes the same conclusions about cultural shifts implied in *Futurecast* by George Barna. Olson states that the church needs to learn to operate under these three assumptions:

> ➤ the world used to be Christian but it is now post-Christian.
> ➤ the world used to be modern but it is now post-modern.
> ➤ the world used to be monoethnic but it is now multiethnic.

Pastor David Platt's book *Radical* challenges the church to dramatically impact today's world climate by understanding that the promise of satisfaction in Christ has been exchanged for the "American Dream." In his book, *Don't Waste your Life*, John Piper echoes the sentiment of Platt by encouraging individuals to find joy, pleasure, and the lasting fulfillment man truly desires by seeking the will of God.

In the book, *Survey of 20th Century Revival Movements,* Richard Riss reveals how in the twentieth century there was a shift in the impact of the revivals because of the shift to a more post-Christian culture, conflicting against the Christian ideology. Francis Schaeffer's book entitled, *The Church at the End of the 20th Century,* looked at the competing revivals in non-Christian thought engulfing the country, and sent out a call to action for Christians to not compromise biblical truth for the popular lies society was embracing.

Making Sense of the Church by Wayne Grudem, and Mark Dever's book *Nine Marks of a Healthy Church* further expand on what the church must have in order to construct a healthy biblically-based structure and operational system. *Perimeters of Light* by Elmer Towns and Ed Stetzer also maps out a foundation upon which a church can grow and develop.[3]

Professionals in North America metropolises are a vital and critical part of the social, economical, and cultural backbone of the workplace contributing much to the material prosperity of society. In general, professionals work long hours to make their businesses and careers meaningful for their personal lives and to become financially independent and secure. These professionals spend their time away from work with family for entertainment or recreation, for personal development or continuing education, hobbies, physical development, and involvement in service clubs, but rarely with religious organizations.

This population group has been influenced by the worldview with its denial of absolutes and a motivation for pure personal gratification. Larry Crabb describes in his book, *Real Church,* how the individualistic theology common today has influenced churches and ministries with a non-biblical contemporary world view:

> "The true Church is not to deal directly with communities, states, and nations but with the individual. Our present and self-serving interests, whether material or spiritual, must be met first. Then we will be able to help others. The great question is not how to serve God in this world by serving others like Jesus did, but how to get God to serve us in this world, by making either our lives comfortably blessed or our souls joyfully spiritual."[4]

This individualistic approach influenced by a non-Christian philosophy of life has permeated our society. As a business professional for the past thirty years, I have amassed a lifetime of experience concerning the personal and workplace challenges Christian professionals encounter today. It has birthed within me a desire to develop effective and practical methods to reach this group for God. These methods include contemporary approaches to evangelism, discipleship, and church growth which follow the Great Commission command to make disciples who are taught to observe the teachings of Christ.

God has called me to follow in the steps of the Apostle Paul as a consulting engineer (tent builder) and minister of the gospel to reach urban professionals worldwide. This book is designed to be the groundwork for a new ministry to fulfill the call to proclaim His glorious name and minister to urban professionals in North America and abroad.

Chapter 1

The Professionals Mission Field

"The world is desperately seeking someone to follow: That they will follow someone is certain, but will that person be one who knows the way of Christ, or will he or she be one like themselves leading them only on into greater darkness?" (Robert E. Coleman, *The Master Plan of Evangelism*)

The professionals mission field has not been widely reached with existing evangelism and discipleship methods. The need exists for believers, who are also professionals, to live beyond themselves and know that future generations will bear the fruit of our witness for Christ to other professionals in metropolises. One of the last commands given by Jesus to his disciples is commonly known as the Great Commission as stated in Matthew 28:19-20, "Go therefore and make disciples of all the nations, baptizing them in the name of the Father and the Son and the Holy Spirit, teaching them to observe all that I commanded you."

The Directive

This directive is an order by Jesus to proclaim His message to reach all mankind in the Church age. John Piper in his book, *Let the Nations be Glad,* describes the emphasis of the call to give all glory and honor to God:

"God is pursuing with omnipotent passion a worldwide purpose of gathering joyful worshipers for himself from every tribe and tongue and people and nation. He has an inexhaustible enthusiasm for the supremacy of his name among the nations. Therefore, let us bring our affections into line with his, and for the sake of his name, let us renounce the quest for worldly comforts and join his global purpose. If we do this, God's omnipotent commitment to his name will be over us like a banner, and we will not lose, is spite of many tribulations (Acts 9:16; Romans 8:35-29). Missions is not the ultimate goal of the church. Worship is. Missions exist because worship doesn't. The Great Commission is first to "delight yourself in the Lord" (Psalm 37:4) and then to declare, "Let the nations be glad and sing for joy" (Psalm 67:4). In this way, God will be glorified from beginning to end, and worship will empower the missionary enterprise until the coming of the Lord."[5]

A review of biblical theology finds the job of the Church and its missionology is to focus on proclaiming the gospel of the Kingdom of God by word and deed to all. David Horton writes about the Old and New Testament axioms for missions which provide emphasis on how life and its purpose for each human and Creation is to give God all glory and honor.

The Old Testament axioms are:
1) God is sovereign in His kingship.
2) God seeks personal commitment from his people.
3) God's people are to constitute a serving community among the nations by example and personal outreach.
4) God's purpose through his people is relentlessly opposed by the inveteracy of human evil and the implacable hostility of Satan and his hosts.
5) God's purpose for Israel and the nations always moves beyond present matters and is invariably directed toward his future and ultimate triumph in history."[6]

The New Testament axioms are:
1) God's sovereignty focuses on Christ's lordship.
2) Christ's lordship demands personal commitment.
3) The community of the King is the body of Christ.
4) The church is called to missions.
5) Obedience to missions involves suffering.
6) The future remains bright with hope when God's redemptive purpose will be fulfilled (Acts 1:8)." [7]

The call of God and its purpose can be also summed up as God is reconciling the world to Himself through Jesus Christ (Matthew 24:14), God is bringing all things together under one head – Jesus Christ (Ephesians 1:9-10), and God is bringing all people to worship Him.[8] Therefore, there is no doubt that God wants us to glorify His name by providing all mankind the opportunity to join Him in seeing His glory fill the heavens and earth.

In his series of books that outline a practical approach to evangelism and discipleship: *The Master Plan of Evangelism*, *The Master Plan for Discipleship*, and *The Master's Way of Personal Evangelism*, Robert E. Coleman emphasized the timeless cry of the human soul to have a fellowship with its Creator. While methods will vary, the priority and aim of evangelism and discipleship is helping others develop a closer walk with God.

In *The Master's Way of Personal Evangelism*, Coleman examines Christ's example, reaching people despite human and environmental limitations. All Jesus asked of His followers was to have faith and act in obedience to God's will for their individual lives. The paths can be different for each person, but the direction in which they are moving should be the same.

The Great Commission leads people to Christ and then they are able to continue their walk with Him. *On Mission with God: Living God's Purpose for His Glory* by Henry Blackaby explains we need to get on mission with God's vision through exercising the disciplines of intercessory prayer, working in the community, working towards racial reconciliation in a business setting, and getting involved or working in ministry.

In the book, *Let the Nations be Glad* by John Piper, he takes a fresh look at the missions ministry in the 21st century by emphasizing one does not necessarily need to go across the globe to reach the people of the world. It is the individual Christian's responsibility to walk with Christ growing a heart and passion to reach the lost world directly around him. When the pursuit of Christ is seen as the highest duty of the individual, the fulfillment of the Great Commission will follow.

In the book *Futurecast,* George Barna examines changes in current trends in attitudes and behaviors in light of a Christian worldview. Barna sees that there is a shrinking level of patience as people shift from a delayed gratification to an instant gratification mindset. Compounding the challenges arising from a changing culture in a hurting economic environment which affects the way people focus their time and energy.

⸺ Key Insight: When the pursuit of Christ is seen as the highest duty of the individual, the fulfillment of the Great Commission will follow.

God's Plan for Professionals

The Great Commission is an obligation that falls upon the whole community of faith with no exceptions. Thus, professionals such as: physicians, school teachers, theologians, engineers and certified public accountants, along with automobile mechanics, home makers, and carpenters are part of His work. This means God wants professionals to make disciples by focusing on biblical principles so the correct methods are used in the outreach for their particular peer group.

Stan Guthrie explains in his book, *Missions in the Third Millennium,* "If the Scriptures say anything about what constitutes obedience to the Great Commission, they say Christ's followers are, at a minimum, to 'make disciples' (Matthew 28:19). For missionaries and Christians to make a lasting impact in the twenty-first century, they will have to give up splashy and ineffective campaigns and refocus their efforts on the essentials of the faith." [9]

The intent is the same for the methods to reach professionals. Robert Coleman speaks of the roles that all believers have regarding the responsibility they ought to take in their lives as followers of Christ in obedience to the Great Commission in his book, *The Master Plan of Discipleship*, where he states:

> "The establishment of a professional clergy has had a sharp effect on the average unordained Christian. The creation of such roles has tended to confuse the priesthood of all believers and has nullified a sense of responsibility for ministry. Many Christians feel quite satisfied with the situation, content to allow paid clergymen and staff to do all the work. But even those who are more sensitive to their calling and want to be involved may experience a sense of frustration as they try to find their place of service. 'After all,' they may ask, 'if I'm not a preacher or missionary or something of the kind, how can I be properly engaged in ministry?' The answer lies in their seeing the Great Commission as lifestyles encompassing the total resources of every child of God. Here the ministry of Christ comes alive in the day-by-day activity of discipline. Whether we have a secular job or an ecclesiastical position, a Christ-like commitment to bring the nations into the eternal Kingdom should be a part of it."[10]

꙳ Key Insight: The Great Commission is an obligation that falls upon the whole community of faith with no exceptions.

God's Business Is the Only Business

Several Bible passages such as Matthew 28:16-20, Mark 16:14-18, Luke 24:46-49, and Acts 1:6-8 clearly state the will of God for believers, professionals, and others to obey the Great Commission.

This obedience requires believers to understand their responsibility today in the context of eternity. This understanding will turn into a proactive approach to serve God and reach all people groups with effective methods. Coleman explains, "Our Lord's command is a summons to live with the same sense of purpose that directed His steps. He has given us in His lifestyle a personal example of what the mandates involves, while the Acts of the Apostles relates that pattern in

His church. Though the principles must be clothed with relevant applications in our contemporary situation, they offer us some guidelines to follow. If they are true, then we are obligated to implement them. When we move from ideas to action, the rubber meets the road."[11]

> **Key Insight: When we move from ideas to action, the rubber meets the road.**

Professionals go about their business everyday according to their field of expertise, but the Christian professional's overarching purpose ought to be to do God's business within the context of their day. They are to fulfill their daily activities according to the specific call by God in each of their lives. There is an urgency for each professional believer to bear Christ's name among non-believing professionals and make use of the time to work diligently for Him. As Horatius Bonar quoted John 9:4 in his book *Words to Winners of Souls*, "We must work while it is day; the night cometh when no man can work." [12]

> ✓**Action Challenge: There is an urgency for each professional believer to bear Christ's name among non-believing professionals, and make use of the time to work diligently for Him.**

The example of teaching formally educated individuals and scholars of the common day is not a new concept and there are examples of apostles teaching professionals from which we may model our ministries. Because Paul came from a professional and trade background himself, his teaching ministry was able to reach not only a wide range of people groups, but specifically his fellow professionals in an effective way. In Acts 16 God uses Paul's sermon to reach and open the heart of a local professional businesswoman, Lydia. She was an influential woman. Her coming to faith in Christ allowed her to lead all of those within her realm of influence to the knowledge of God as well.

Mankind has found itself in a continuous state of change since the beginning of the human race when God created Adam and Eve. Therefore, understanding of the social, economic, cultural, demographic, technological, and other related variables in the environment in which they live and work are important in the development of evangelism and discipleship methods to reach professionals.

We will delve further into this in upcoming chapters, but first take the time to review the key insights gleaned from this chapter and begin to put them into practice in your own life.

✎ Key Insights from Chapter 1

- The world is desperately seeking someone to follow.
- When we move from ideas to action, the rubber meets the road.
- Exemplifying the pursuit of Christ brings fulfillment of the Great Commission.
- The Great Commission falls upon the whole community of faith with no exceptions.

✓ Action Challenge from Chapter 1

Each professional believer is to bear Christ's name among non-believing professionals.

- Will you take up the challenge and begin to exemplify your belief in God in all of your day-to-day activities?
- List some ways you can do this more effectively especially among your workplace peers.

Chapter 2

Understanding the Urban Professional Environment

Do not love the world or the things in the world. If anyone loves the world, the love of the Father is not in him. For all that is in the world, the lust of the flesh and the lust of the eyes and the boastful pride of life, is not from the Father, but is from the world. The world is passing away, and also its lusts; but the one who does the will of God lives forever. (1 John 2:15-17)

There is a growing need in society for individuals to obtain a certain level of education so they can remain competitive in the growing global economy. This is becoming even more relevant in the metropolitan areas. As economic growth brings about the presence of more professionals in the workplace, it is becoming more important for the church to develop programs which can meet these business professionals' spiritual needs. Cultures, worldviews, and philosophies of life are shaped through the education received in an academic setting for most of these professionals. Believers must be well versed in these areas to effectively evangelize their peers and counter unbiblical mindsets.

One can assume that most professionals in United States metropolises fall into the middle or wealthy social class of American society based on economic earnings alone. Ruby K. Payne in her book, *A Framework for Understanding Poverty*, analyzes the mindset of the people who have higher income levels and those who do not. There are general personality and psycho-social characteristics that have been designated for each economic class: low, middle, and wealthy. By understanding the psycho-social characteristics we are able to examine by class the basic trends. This background can provide more insight into the mindset of the working professional population.

A middle class individual has his social emphasis in self-governance and self-sufficiency. He invests his time in improving his language skills through formal education. This way he will be able to better negotiate opportunities to climb the ladder of success and make money. He believes that his destiny is based on the choices he makes and good choices will change his future! The driving force is his belief that if he works hard, he will achieve success. He spends time considering his future retirement and decisions are made based on future ramifications. He feels love and acceptance is conditional and largely based upon achievement. He values things and feels money is to be managed wisely. The clothing he wears is valued for its quality and its acceptance into the norm of middle class, labels are important. He likes to eat quality food and a key question is: "Did you like it?" He sees the world in terms of national settings and likes to use humor when facing unpleasant or unknown situations.

Individuals in the wealthy social class emphasize social exclusions. They invest their time in traditions and history. They feel education is a necessary tradition for making and maintaining connections. They use formal register in their language for language is about networking. Their decisions are made partially on the basis of tradition and decorum. They believe their destiny is noblesse oblige. Their driving force is their financial, political, and social connections. They feel love and acceptance are conditional and related to social standing and connections. They value one-of-a-kind objects, legacies, and pedigrees. They value clothing for its artistic sense and expression. Designer labels are important. How their food is presented is very important! Their humor is about social faux pas.[13]

On the other hand, non-professionals may mostly fall in the poverty to middle class social levels – the levels who most populate our current churches. One of their characteristics is they prefer to socialize with people they like, they value education, and revere it as an abstract but not as a reality. Their language is casual and it is about survival. To them the present is the most important factor of life and decisions are made for the moment based on feelings or survival. They believe in fate and that they cannot do much to mitigate chance. Their most valuable possession is the people they relate with. Love and acceptance are conditional, based upon whether the individual is liked. Their family structure tends to be matriarchal and they like to use humor about people and sex.[14]

21st Century Church Trends in North America

There are many new challenges being faced by the church in this century as this "new millennium sees a radically changing world of economic upheavals, political uncertainties, overwhelming technological innovations, and fundamental changes to centuries-old social, ethical, and religious values."[15] Since the call of God to His church is a global enterprise, there is a need to understand the major global trends which have significant consequences in how each is carried out. David Horton, editor of *The Portable Seminary,* presents the following current trends:

1) Increasing globalization is the phenomena of having the same factors and events influencing people worldwide.
2) Increasing clash of civilizations such as Western, Orthodox, Latin American, Islamic, Hindi, Japanese, and African create conflicts.
3) Increasing persecution indicates more than 200 million in over sixty nations are being denied basic human rights because of their Christian faith.
4) Increasing secularism is shown when public expressions of faith are not tolerated.
5) Increasing post modernism means that knowledge is not objective and there are no absolutes. Truth is considered to be dependent upon the community in which it resides and not established by the sovereign Creator.
6) There is an increasing gap between poor and rich.
7) There is an increasing impact of HIV/AIDS.
8) There is an increasing number of children at risk around the world who are on the street and without family support.

9) There is an increasing number of refugees due to the reality of persecution, war, famine, and hopelessness that has made millions run in hope of a new life.
10) There has been an increasing number of Christians in non-Western countries.
11) There has been an increasing number of missionaries from younger sending countries.

This changing world has affected the makeup of North American metropolises due to this world immigration.[16]

21st Century Society Trends in North America

> **Key Insight: Society has become increasingly narcissistic and developed a lack of patience in the culture where needs are met immediately.**

George Barna has been integrating information of the church and secular culture in North American since 1984. He has become an often quoted person because of the depth and applicability of his group research work. Several of today's trends are found in his book, *Futurecast,* which is an extensive new research on how behaviors, attitudes, and beliefs are shaping society's future.[17] Barna states, "America is undergoing significant changes, and the nature of those changes is both complex and chaotic. The historical foundations on which our society was developed are facing some severe challenges."[18]

In his research, Barna also found Americans have increased their stress levels and strive to alleviate it with an addiction to media. The typical adult allocates more than fifty hours per week to media absorption. The study also discovered how the concept of common good, "sacrificing a personal benefit of opportunity to advance the good of the community,"[19] is not part of a society that has become increasingly narcissistic. There is also a marked lack of patience in the culture where needs are met immediately.

Barna summarizes his findings about society's critical shifts in values and attitudes in the following table which also shows most professionals approach to their personal life and business:

Table: Critical Shifts in Values and Attitudes[20]	
What We Used to Embrace	**What we Now Embrace**
Excellence	Adequacy
Optimism	Pessimism
Common Good	Individual Advantage
Delayed Gratification	Instant Gratification
Respect	Inactivity
Christian God	Amorphous God
Truth	Skepticism
Heroes	Celebrities
Knowledge	Experience

Why Don't People Go to Church?

➥ **Key Insight: There has been a decrease in feelings about the church, a move away from Christianity, and a decrease in religious activity.**

Thom Schultz visited the topic of why people do not go to church anymore using a simple qualitative interview-based research process to answer this timeless question. The author staked out a local city park and interviewed randomly selected individuals of mixed population.

Four common answers emerged from this research and revolved around people's misunderstanding of what it means to be a Christian.

Church people judge me.
I don't want to be lectured.
They're a bunch of hypocrites.
I don't want religion I want God.[21]

Church people judge me. With the way society is trending, people have an uncertain feeling of conviction since they are not absolutely sure what the conviction is based on. Without a foundation in the Word of God as the absolute truth, they have no moral compass.

I don't want to be lectured. People are more self-assure because they are confident in any defiant behavior they may be practicing and do not want to be told it is wrong since they are entrapped by the very act they do not want revealed.

They're a bunch of hypocrites. People use this simple excuse to transfer blame onto another person.

I don't want religion I want God. The final common answer shows that there is a healthy craving for something larger than the human race. There is a thirst for spirituality in the professional urban population. Unfortunately, due to a misunderstanding of what biblical Christianity is, people look for other ways to satisfy this spiritual hunger.[22]

Over the past five years people have not given much thought to their religious beliefs, practices or preferences. There has been a decrease in feelings about the church, a shift to move away from Christianity, and a decrease in religious activity.[23] This apathy and discontent towards the church raises questions of the effectiveness of current church programming. Research also shows that most religious behaviors and beliefs are formed by the age of thirteen and little happens after that. Adults show little changes in religious thinking possibly because there is not a variety of attractive programming for adults available in the church community.

There are still churches which are impacting the community, but generally there has been a shift in the effectiveness of the church on the surrounding community. The Barna Group research found that only a little over half of the people who went to church felt a connection with God while there, and 61% of churchgoers could not remember an important new insight or understanding related to their faith gained by attending church. 26% of the Americans who went to church said their life was changed greatly by attending church while 46% said that their lives have not been changed greatly by attending church.[24]

David Olson's book, *The American Church in Crisis*, states research based on a national database of over 200,000 churches found that "17.5 percent of the population attended an orthodox Christian church on a weekend in 2005. Non-orthodox Christian churches and non-Christian religions add an additional 35,000 houses of worship while increasing the 2005 attendance percentage to 19.5 percent."[25] Furthermore, research shows that in no single state did church attendance keep up with the population growth, 795 counties did against 2,303 which did not.[26]

The Professional Career Dream in North America

Professionals have invested years into higher education and training in their profession to achieve their professional status. Medical Doctors, Lawyers, Professional Engineers, Chaplains, Doctors of Physical Therapy, Certified Public Accountants or Dentists have reached a social level and financial lifestyle which helps them achieve personal, family and business success, and satisfaction in which God has not been a priority.

David Platt in his book, *Radical*, describes how people have changed the version of the Jesus of the Bible to accommodate their current view of the life in North America.

> "A nice, middle-class, American Jesus doesn't mind materialism and would never call us to give away everything we have. A nice American Jesus would not expect us to forsake our closest relationships so that he receives all our affection. A nice American Jesus is fine with nominal devotion that does not infringe on our comforts, because, after all, he loves us just the way we are. A nice American Jesus wants us to be balanced, and to avoid danger altogether while he brings comfort and prosperity as we live our Christian spin on the American dream.[27]

This view has hindered the priorities of professionals who are believers. If they do not invest to make God their joy instead of their possessions, the important work of the church and its missions are affected. In his book, *Missions in the Third Millennium*, Guthrie states: "Thanks to incessant media bombardment, we know that an initial investment of $10,000.00, earning an average of 12 percent annually, would become $930,510.00 in 40 years."[28] That being so, the difficult decision to give money to missions becomes all harder. Who in his right mind would give up the multiplicative power of compound interest? Viewed this way, every dollar given away instead of invested really is sacrificial. When you consider the cost of retirement, college education or that small vacation home they have always dreamed about, a $10,000.00 gift can be seen as a million dollar loss. Whether fueled by the delayed gratification mindset of the baby boomers or the instant gratification mindset prevalent now, the bottom line is that effective mission programs need to open the hearts of professionals to understand that sacrificing for the Kingdom of God is not taking away from their God given personal joys, achievements, or goals. Supporting missions, whether with time or money, is the result of a calling by Christ and a shift away from a worldly mindset, and not a superficial sense of obligation.

✓**Action Challenge: Your ultimate goal is to allow God to reveal Himself to you and then through you to others.**

Our Mission with God

God created the Universe and each of the human beings in existence for a reason and purpose according to His sovereign plan. He is not interested in just giving us a life experience. Believers are to experience a life with Him in order to fulfill His sovereign purpose for His glory and honor for all eternity. Willis and Blackaby describe this purpose in their book, *On Mission with God:*

> "God reveals Himself to you so you can adjust your life to Him and join Him on His mission. Where He takes you is His doing, not ours. He wants to reveal His glory to a waiting world through you. He can do it anywhere He chooses when you allow Him to manifest Himself through you. As you experience God's mission you do not choose your experiences, your assignment or location. He does. Your ultimate goal is to allow God to reveal Himself to you and then through you to others."[29]

A great example of a professional who pursued the presence of God and used his vocational skills to honor and glorify God while growing the church is found in the life of Hudson Taylor. In the 19th century, Hudson Taylor used his skills as a physician and answered the God-given call to bring the gospel to China. The autobiography of Hudson Taylor gives the professional of today a hope and example to follow in living a life after God's will.

"God made us so that we could reflect His glory back to Him. Glory is to God as wet is to water, as heat is to fire, as light is to bulb. Glory is what emanates from God. Although we can't see God (1 John 4:12), we can see His glory in creation and in His people when they model His holiness. Glory is the evidence that God is present. God's purpose in your life is to bring glory to or display Himself. In fact, He wants to do it even in the most mundane things that you do. "Whether…you eat or drink or whatever you do, do all to the glory of God" say 1 Corinthians 10:31. In commanding us to glorify Him, God invites us to leave His fingerprints on everything we touch."[30] (James MacDonald, *Gripped by the Greatness of God*)

Take the time to review the key insights gleaned from this chapter and begin to put them into practice in your own life.

☙ Key Insights from Chapter 2

- There has been a decrease in feelings about the church. Society has become increasingly narcissistic and lacks patience. There has been a move away from Christianity and a decrease in religious activity. An American Jesus is fine with nominal devotion that does not infringe on our comforts.

✓Action Challenge from Chapter 2

Your ultimate goal is to allow God to reveal Himself to you and then through you to others.

- Write your description of who Jesus is and what He expects from you as His disciple.
- How much of this are you doing in your life right now?
- What do you need to do to truly allow God to reveal Himself through you to others?
- Consider to start doing it today.

Chapter 3

Past and Current Trends in Reaching Professionals

Therefore be careful how you walk, not as unwise men but as wise, making the most of your time, because the days are evil. So then do not be foolish, but understand what the will of the Lord is. (Ephesians 5:15-17)

Paul's approach for reaching the scholars of his day gives believers a foundation for and shows the importance of a respectful approach in sharing the gospel of Christ in a well-articulated and uncompromising manner. Acts 24:1-23 and Acts 26:1-26 tell the story of Paul's imprisonment and trial. Throughout the hardship of imprisonment, God is glorified in the testimony and manner in which Paul conducts himself in sharing the Gospel message.

> **Key Insight: In the post-Christian world, pastors, churches, and Christians need to operate more as the early church did.**

The North American church experienced a change with the culture during the transition from the last millennium to this 21st century. Olson describes three critical transitions that have taken placed during this period:

1) Our world used to be Christian, but it is now becoming post-Christian.
2) Our world used to be modern, but it is now becoming post modern.
3) Our world used to be monoethnic, but it is now becoming multiethnic.[31]

The above changes lead to a different approach to Christian ministries which requires the following mindset:

- In the post-Christian world, pastors, churches, and Christians need to operate more as the early church did.
- In the post-Christian world the needs of outsiders become most important. Ministry is more like missionary work with a renewed emphasis on the message and mission of Jesus.
- The role of pastors is to lead the church in this mission outside of the church.
- In the post-Christian world, only the healthy, mission-minded church will prosper.
- This is not an issue of traditional versus contemporary style of ministry. That perspective is a dated dichotomy from the 1980s and 1990s that no longer is meaningful.
- Churches must develop a mission mind-set, going out into the world to meet people's needs.[32]

During the 19th century, North America experienced several revival movements that exalted the name of God by proclaiming the message of the gospel and reaching the society groups of this time. Riss' book, *A Survey of 20th Century Revivals Movements in North America,* describes how the 20th century revivals had a different impact from those which took placed in the 19th century:

"Prior to the twentieth century, revival usually had a tremendous impact upon society bringing about the advancement of important humanitarian causes and resulting in significant social reforms. Because of the more limited scope of the twentieth-century revivals, such effects were less pronounced. A much smaller proportion of the population was involved in such movements in the twentieth century due to the shifts in world view that had taken place in Western culture as a whole."³³

A Case Against the World

Understanding postmodern philosophy is critical if effective evangelism and discipleship methods are to be developed in reaching professionals. The philosophy and practical approach to life for many professionals is based on modernism and postmodernism. The definitions from John MacArthur's book, *The Truth War*, need to be considered:

> **Modernism** was characterized by the belief that truth exists and that the scientific method is the only reliable way to determine that truth. In the so-called "modern" era, most academic disciplines (philosophy, science, literature, and education) were driven primarily by rationalistic presuppositions. Modern thought treated human reason as the final arbiter of what is true, discounted the idea of the supernatural, and looked for scientific and rationalistic explanations for everything.³⁴

> **Postmodernism** in general is marked by a tendency to dismiss the possibility of any sure and settled knowledge of the truth and suggests that if objective truth exists, it cannot be known with any degree of certainty because the subjectivity of the human mind makes knowledge of objective truth impossible. So it is useless to think of truth in objective terms. Objectivity is an illusion. Nothing is certain, and the thoughtful person will never speak with too much conviction about anything. Strong convictions about any point of truth are judged supremely arrogant and hopelessly naive. Everyone is entitled to his own truth.³⁵

> ᛞ **Key Insight:** "The postmodern view of life has resulted in a widespread rejection of truth and the enshrinement of skepticism in which trust claims are despised." (John MacArthur) ³⁶

The ideologies in today's society require Christians to use the power of God and the Bible as their offensive tools and defensive weapons to confront these culturally embedded views. The methods to reach the professionals are not carnal. They are not about battles for lands, personality conflicts, denominational issues, or skirmishes over material possessions. It is a spiritual battle using good works to proclaim the Truth of God.[37] MacArthur explains: "Confront the spirit of a relativistic age and diligently apply ourselves to the unfailing Word of God. Discernment will come only as we train our minds to be understanding in the truth of God's Word and learn to apply that truth skillfully to our lives."[38]

> ✓ **Action Challenge: The ideologies in today's society require Christians to use the power of God and the Bible as their offensive tools and defensive weapons to confront these culturally embedded views.**

A Case for Christian Apologetics

> **Key Insight: The methods to reach professionals will address the existence of God by sharing why Christianity is reasonable.**

Professionals will ask questions about life that are consequential to their existence. Where did we come from? Who are we? Why are we here? How should we live? Where are we going? The answers depend on the existence of God. If He exists there is meaning and purpose in life. On the other hand, if there is no God, life will mean nothing at the end with no purpose, right or wrong and therefore, it does not matter how they live or believe.[39] The methods to reach professionals will address the existence of God by sharing why Christianity is reasonable. Norman Geisler describes the intellectual objections, emotional obstacles, and volitional reasons that will impede evangelism to professionals.

> ➢ First, there are many perceived **intellectual objections** like the problem of evil, and the objections of many scientists.

- ➤ Second, there are **emotional obstacles** that sometimes obstruct the acceptance of Christianity. Christian exclusivism, the doctrine of hell, and the hypocrisy of Christians are emotional roadblocks to just about everyone. (In fact, hypocrisy in the church probably repels people more than any other factor. Someone once said the biggest problem with Christianity is Christians!)
- ➤ Finally, there are **volitional reasons** to reject Christianity, namely Christian morality which seems to restrict our choices in life. Since most of us don't want to answer to anyone, yielding our freedom to an unseen God is not something we naturally want to do.[40]

Professionals question the person of Jesus as God and the claim that the Bible is the inspired Word of God. The line of reasoning used by Geisler in his book "The Twelve Points that Show Christianity is True" is an example of how to present a case for Christianity to professionals which proceeds logically from the concept of truth all the way to the conclusion that the Bible is the Word of God:[41]

1) Truth about reality is knowable.
2) The opposite of true is false.
3) It is true the theistic God exists evidenced by the:
   a) Beginning of the universe (Cosmological Argument)
   b) Design of the universe (Teleological Argument/Anthropic Principle)
   c) Design of life (Teleological Argument)
   d) Moral Law (Moral Argument)
4) If God exists then miracles are possible.
5) Miracles can be used to confirm a message from God (i.e., as acts of God to confirm a word from God).
6) The New Testament is historically reliable evidenced by authentic, eyewitness testimony.
7) The New Testament says Jesus claimed to be God.
8) Jesus' claim to be God was miraculously confirmed by:
   a) His fulfillment of many prophecies about Himself
   b) His sinless life and miraculous deeds

c) His prediction and accomplishment of His resurrection
9) Therefore Jesus is God.
10) Whatever Jesus (who is God) teaches is true.
11) Jesus taught that the Bible is the Word of God.
12) Therefore, it is true that the Bible is the Word of God (and anything opposed to it is false.)

Norman Geisler states, "Inerrancy means that when all facts are known, the Scriptures in their original autographs and properly interpreted will be shown to be wholly true in everything that they affirm, whether that has to do with doctrine or morality or with the social, physical or life sciences."[42]

This implies that inerrancy:

o applies equally to all parts of the Scriptures as originally written
o is intimately tied up with the science of biblical interpretation
o is related to Scripture's intention
o does not demand strict adherence to the rules of grammar
o does not exclude use of figures of speech or literary genre
o does not demand historical or semantic precision or the technical language of modern science
o does not required verbal exactness in the citation of the Old Testament by the New
o does not demand that the sayings of Jesus contain the exact words of Jesus, only the exact voice
o does not guarantee the exhaustive comprehensiveness of any single account or of combined accounts where these are involved
o does not demand the infallibility or inerrancy of the non-inspired sources used by biblical writers
o no doctrine of inerrancy can determine in advance the solution to individual or specific problem passages
o it is a doctrine that must be asserted but which may not be demonstrated with respect to all phenomena of Scripture.[43]

The User-Friendly Church Approach

☞ Key Insight: Methods to reach professionals must confront the pragmatic philosophy approach and avoid falling into the trap of the current market-driven ministry trend which is not a God driven ministry.

Professionals in urban metropolises follow a cultural trend which was popularized at the end of the 19th century by philosopher and psychologist William James along with other noted intellectuals such as John Dewey and George Santayana. James gave this philosophy a name: Pragmatism. John MacArthur describes James' work content and its effect in our society:

> The final chapter of his book was titled "Pragmatism and Religion." In it, he essentially acknowledged that faith and pragmatism are contradictory values. Pragmatism, to James' way of thinking, argues decisively for pluralism of religion (276-278). Modern and postmodern pragmatists have moved toward the same condition.[44]

MacArthur defines pragmatism as "the notion that meaning or worth is determined by practical consequences. It is closely akin to utilitarianism, the belief that usefulness is the standard of what is good. To a pragmatist/utilitarian, if a technique or course of action has the desired effect, it is good. If it doesn't seem to work, it must be wrong."[45]

This philosophical mindset is rooted in the professional's approach to life and business where results are measured in financial profit and achievements, and by running and being ahead in business and personal life.

✓ Action Challenge: Pastors must resist the temptation to tailor their messages to the whims and short attention spans of drive-by listeners. Catering to the sound bite surfer is the surest way to empty one's message of real substance.

Professionals find themselves in the pursuit of success and not excellence. There is a drive to have success in this world. Therefore, some ministries adopt a market driven, user friendly approach in which the goal is to give people what they want. Ministers many times do not declare God's demands to people, but adapt to what the people's demands are, doing whatever is needed to cater to the opinion of the public.[46]

Today's customer-driven mentality is such that it does not matter what the principles and values are because as customers, they have the right to demand those who give them services and products meet their expectations. MacArthur furthers adds to this idea when he says, "and with so many options, the most casual customer has achieved ultimate sovereignty. If he doesn't like what he sees, he can simply change the channel. Pastors must resist the temptation to tailor their messages to the whims and short attention spans of drive-by listeners like that. Catering to the sound bite surfer is the surest way to empty one's message of real substance."[47]

Professionals find that user friendliness has led to non-biblical based teachings, such as the conditional immortality which is the idea that unredeemed sinners are simply eradicated rather than spending eternity in hell.[48] A 2002 article on the front page of the Los Angeles Times indicated that "one of the most popular movements afoot today embraces a doctrine known as 'conditional immortality,' similar to annihilations. It is the idea that unredeemed sinners are simply eradicated rather than spending eternity in hell. A perfect fit for the user-friendly philosophy, this view teaches that a merciful God could not possibly consign created beings to eternal torment. Instead, he obliterates them completely."[49]

> ✓**Action Challenge: The answer, of course, is not an unfriendly church, but a vibrant, loving, honest, committed, worshiping fellowship of believers who minister to one another like the church in Acts 4 – who eschew sin, keep one another accountable, and boldly proclaim the full truth of Scripture.**

The methods to reach professionals can not follow the presented user friendly approach but must be God friendly.

"Too many who have embraced the user-friendly trend have not carefully pondered how user-friendliness is incompatible with true biblical theology. It is, at its heart, a pragmatic, not a biblical, outlook. It is based on precisely the kind of thinking that is eating away at the heart of orthodox doctrine. It is leading evangelism into neo-modernism and putting churches in the fast lane on the down-grade. The answer, of course, is not an unfriendly church, but a vibrant, loving, honest, committed, worshiping fellowship of believers who minister to one another like the church in Acts 4 – but who eschew sin, keep one another accountable, and boldly proclaim the full truth of Scripture. People who have no love for the things of God may not find such a place very user-friendly. (John MacArthur, *Ashamed of the Gospel*)[50]

Current Methods Reaching Professionals in North America Metropolis

Several ministries addressing the workplace and business owners are in existence in North America today. Following are examples of ministers or ministries reaching professionals even though they do not necessarily focus their evangelism and discipleship efforts on urban professionals exclusively.

John Piper is the pastor at Bethlehem Baptist Church in Twin Cities, Minnesota, and has been a voice for reaching the people of the world through his bestselling works over the past several decades. Piper has written over forty books and has over thirty years of experience in preaching and teaching aimed at reaching many people groups. Many professionals attend and are members of Bethlehem Baptist Church.

Marketplace Ministries is specifically geared towards the reaching and developing of Christian business leaders in their specific lines of work and who already know Christ as their personal Lord and Savior. The intent is to equip these leaders with the necessary tools to live out their faith and develop a Kingdom purpose for their business. The precepts of this ministry are to: discover, develop, and deploy individuals to become marketplace ministers by helping them to understand God's call for their life, by means of monthly small groups, while demonstrating leadership accountability, and by focusing on biblical principles needed to run their businesses from God's perspective. This ministry reaches out in the marketplace to professionals and non-professionals.[51] "Marketplace Ministry's purpose is to create a discipleship and business leadership ministry committed to equipping and developing business leaders to be more effective for God where they are. Individuals meet monthly to learn how to share the gospel in a normal, natural way; how to pray and minister to people; how to walk in intimacy with God throughout their day; and how to hear God and be effectively 'led by the Spirit.'"[52]

Paul Gazelka addresses this ministry concept in his book, *Market Place Ministers,* where he states: "Marketplace ministers are part of how the Lord will reach the people of the earth in these last days. Influential business people interested in proclaiming the gospel will be greatly used by the Lord in world outreach. Marketplace ministers will reach people a professional minister would never be able to touch because of the unique door that will be open to them because they are in business."[53]

City Life Church Life Men's Life Groups are designed to help all men, professionals and nonprofessionals, to have fellowship with God. Their website says: "Take Aim! This is the sentiment that best articulates our men's life groups that meet throughout the year. It is taken from a text found in 1 Corinthians 9:23-27. Paul says that he is not going to run the race of life without aim. There is an intentionality to his life and so should be to ours. In verse 23 he states, 'And I do all things for the sake of the gospel, that I may become a fellow partaker of it!' We also find this concept of taking aim in relation to sin. One of the most common Greek words that translates as sin to English in the New Testament comes from an archery term that means to miss the mark. At City Life, they are committed to helping men take aim at stopping the patterns of sin that are so destructive, fracturing families, eroding their own lives, and missing the mark of their destiny."[54]

The Other Six Day Ministry based in Raleigh, North Carolina, is an interdenominational national discipleship ministry that exists to give glory to God by assisting Christian men and women as they seek to practice their faith in the workplace and in their daily living. The ministry provides daily devotionals and congregational equipping to help people think through and jump-start an understanding of God's Word as it relates to work and the workplace. It also includes pastor led initiatives which include practical methods such as prayer teams, devotionals, and Angel Tree ministry in order to witness to the working place community.[55]

The Downtown Bible Study Ministry in Portland, Oregon is led by Scott Gilchrist, who is the Pastor of Southwest Bible Church. They have formatted a Bible study layout that is geared towards reaching the business people and students of that city. The Bible study group meets once a week in the Portland Art Museum and is also globally broadcast on the radio. The approach to meet in a neutral place makes attendance less intimidating, and provides a spiritually refreshing thirty-minute Bible teaching (non-denominational), an encouraging break in the work week, an opportunity to network by meeting other Christians in the downtown business community, an informal atmosphere to bring friends or co-workers, a complimentary lunch buffet each week, an opportunity to grow deeper in the understanding of God's Word, and practical insight on real life issues. This ministry does not only target professionals, but also the marketplace part of the community in downtown Portland.[56]

The Capitol Hill Baptist Church has a ministry to outreach the mission field of the Capital Hill community within the various age groups using, among other methods, small group discipleship format. This has proven successful in the metropolitan area of Washington, DC, by allowing individuals to grow and develop in a more intimate setting than they would find in corporate worship services on Sunday. It does not have a specific ministry to reach professionals but it does reach the people of this community in which many professionals live.[57]

The C12 Group Ministry is a round table group formed by leading Christian CEOs and business owners that encourages transparency and accountability among like-minded Christian business owners and professionals who are committed to improving their businesses for the advancement of the Kingdom. The approach includes:

1) A Trusted Peer Board which provides the wisdom and insight of a group of business owners in order to keep them focused and accountable to the principles and core values that guide their lives.
2) A Structured Business Curriculum used to discuss best-practice business topics through a Bible-centered lens with a hard-hitting, real world content designed to provide a life-long learning experience.
3) One-on-one Consultants for personalized time to address specific issues in life and business.[58]

The following data table shows that both the ministers and professionals surveyed find that the best-approach to evangelize and disciple professionals is the one-to-one or in small group at workplace or home.

Table: Location Setting Which Works Best to Reach Professionals				
Group Surveyed	One-to-One	Small Group Gathering at Workplace or Home	Large Group Gathering at Workplace or Home	Gathering in a Church Congregation
Ministers	42.3%	34.6%	11.5%	11.5%
Professionals	50.0%	25.0%	15.0%	10.0%

Biblical Principles for the 21st Century Ambassador of Christ

There are many biblical principles which can be cited in reference to ministering to the people of the world, and how Christians must conduct themselves in accomplishing that mission in the 21st century.

☐ **Romans 12:1-2** urges believers to give themselves as a living sacrifice, renew their minds by God's Spirit, and not conform to the mold of the carnal world.

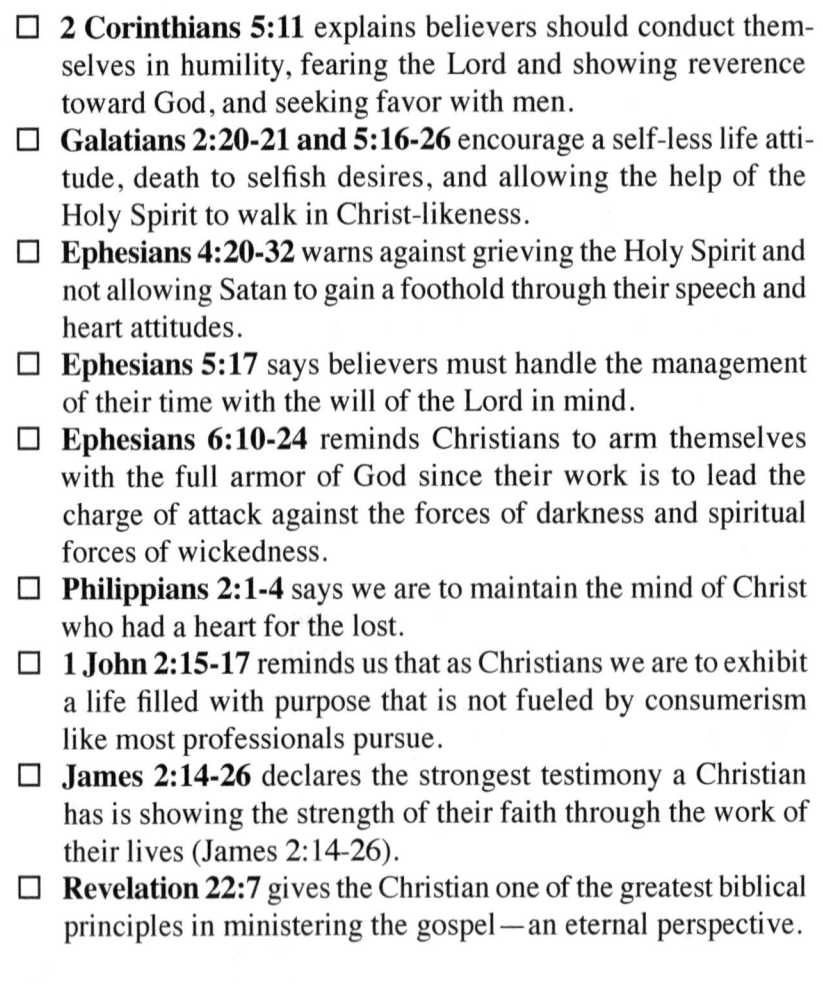

- ☐ **2 Corinthians 5:11** explains believers should conduct themselves in humility, fearing the Lord and showing reverence toward God, and seeking favor with men.
- ☐ **Galatians 2:20-21 and 5:16-26** encourage a self-less life attitude, death to selfish desires, and allowing the help of the Holy Spirit to walk in Christ-likeness.
- ☐ **Ephesians 4:20-32** warns against grieving the Holy Spirit and not allowing Satan to gain a foothold through their speech and heart attitudes.
- ☐ **Ephesians 5:17** says believers must handle the management of their time with the will of the Lord in mind.
- ☐ **Ephesians 6:10-24** reminds Christians to arm themselves with the full armor of God since their work is to lead the charge of attack against the forces of darkness and spiritual forces of wickedness.
- ☐ **Philippians 2:1-4** says we are to maintain the mind of Christ who had a heart for the lost.
- ☐ **1 John 2:15-17** reminds us that as Christians we are to exhibit a life filled with purpose that is not fueled by consumerism like most professionals pursue.
- ☐ **James 2:14-26** declares the strongest testimony a Christian has is showing the strength of their faith through the work of their lives (James 2:14-26).
- ☐ **Revelation 22:7** gives the Christian one of the greatest biblical principles in ministering the gospel—an eternal perspective.

Take the time to review the key insights gleaned from this chapter and begin to put them into practice in your own life.

↵ Key Insights from Chapter 3

- In the post-Christian world, pastors, churches, and Christians need to operate more as the early church did.
- The postmodern view of life has resulted in a widespread rejection of truth and the enshrinement of skepticism in which truth claims are despised. This view says that truth is not fixed and objective, but something individually determined by each

person's unique, subjective perceptions with the intent to eliminate morality and guilt from their lives. As Josh McDowell has argued: *Absolute truth is true for all people, at all times, and in all situations.*
- Methods to reach professionals must confront the pragmatic philosophy approach and avoid falling into the trap of the current market-driven ministry trend which is not a God-driven ministry.

✓ Action Challenges from Chapter 3

- The ideologies in today's society require Christians to use the power of God and the Bible as their offensive tools and defensive weapons to confront these culturally embedded views.

How well equipped are you?
Are you aware of the culturally embedded views you will be called to confront?
Do you know how to effectively combat these views?
Review "The Twelve Points that Show Christianity is True" so that you can use this process as you develop your own strategy.

- We need to confront the spirit of a relativistic age and diligently apply ourselves to the unfailing Word of God. We need to train our minds to be understanding in the truth of God's Word and learn to apply that truth skillfully to our lives.

How are you going to train your mind in the truths of God's Word? Go back and review the Biblical Principles for the 21st Century Ambassador of Christ. Check them off as you read and study them. What new truth did you learn from this chapter and how are you going to begin to apply it to your life?

- We need to keep one another accountable, and boldly proclaim the full truth of Scripture.

Are you part of an accountability group that has determined to boldly proclaim the full truth of the Scripture?
Why is this important for you to do?

Chapter 4

Biblical Principles to Reach Professionals

Oh, the depth of the riches both of the wisdom and knowledge of God! How unsearchable are His judgments and unfathomable His ways! For who has known the mind of the Lord, or who became His counselor? Or who has first given Him that ti might be paid back to Him again? For from Him and through Him and to Him are all things. To Him be the glory forever. Amen. (Romans 11:33-36)

The ministry to reach professionals should consist of a team approach with support between the professionals and local churches. Therefore, an analysis of principles associated with the church, evangelism, and discipleship in order to give the biblical basis and foundation for the ministry methods is necessary. Since the principles associated with the personal relationship between God and each individual will determine the outcome of their life experience during the pilgrimage on the planet Earth and eternity, these too will be discussed.

 Key Insight: Christianity is not about rules though it does have principles. It is about Jesus Christ.

Church Principles

> "It will be impossible for the church of Jesus Christ to revive itself and make a difference for the Savior in this world if it doesn't obey the Great Commission and share its faith. It is imperative that churches face this issue and commit to their God-intended missions." (Aubrey Malphurs, *A New Kind of Church*) [59]

Wayne Grudem's definition of the Church states it "is the Community of All true believers for All Time."[60] This definition includes all those who are saved. The Apostle Paul indicates this purpose from God in Ephesians 5:25, "Christ loved the church and gave himself up for her" (NASB). The Church has directives in terms of ministry to God through worship (Colossians 3:16), ministry to nurture believers (Colossians 1:28), and ministry to the world through evangelism (Matthew 28:19) which must be exercised and balanced in life in order to carry them out effectively. All ministry foundation must be that Christ, who is God, gave His life for the payment of sins so that those who believe and accept Him as Lord and Savior are forgiven and given eternal life.

"Christianity is not about rules though it does have principles. It's about Jesus Christ, and if you are properly related to Him by faith, you're a Christian" (Elmer Towns, *Perimeters of Light*).[61] Ministry must clearly identify the boundaries with the world in what Dr. Towns calls the "perimeters of light":

> The perimeter is not about where the traveler passes from total light to total darkness. A perimeter is a "twilight zone," where it's not completely light, nor is it completely black. Sometimes it's hard to see clearly at the edge of the zone- it's hard to see the edge itself. God knows where Christianity leaves off and the world takes over. Even when you are not sure where the boundary is located, God knows.[62]

Ministry must be pure from wrong doctrine and conduct in order to conform to the revealed will of God to the church and must include:

- Biblical doctrine or right preaching of the Word (Colossians 1:28)
- Proper use of the sacraments or ordinances (1 Corinthians 5:6-7, 12-13)
- Right use of church discipline (Matthew 18:15-17)
- Genuine worship (Ephesians 5:18-20; Colossians 3:16-17)
- Effective prayer (James 5:15, Ephesians 6:18)
- Effective witness (Matthew 28:19-20; John 13:34-35; Acts 2:44-47; I John 4:7)
- Effective fellowship (1 John 1:5-7, Hebrews 10:25)
- Biblical church government (1 Timothy 3:1-13)
- Spiritual power in ministry (Acts 1:8, Romans 1:16, 1 Corinthians 4:20; 2 Corinthians 10:3-4; Galatians 3:3-5; 2 Timothy 3:5; James 5:16)
- Personal holiness of life among members (I Thessalonians 4:3; Hebrews 12:14)
- Care for the poor (Acts 4:32-35; Romans 15:26; Galatians 2:10)
- Love for Christ (1 Peter 1:8; Revelation 2:4)[63]

Grudem further clarifies about the importance of making the church and its ministries pure per the will of God when he states:

> Moreover, Paul told Titus that elders must "be able to give instruction in sound doctrine and also to confront those who contradict it" (Titus 1:9), and he said that false teachers "must be silenced" (Titus 1:11). Jude urged Christians to "contend for the faith which was once for all delivered to the saints" (Jude 3). In fact, all Christians are to "strive to excel in *building up the church*" (I Corinthians 14:12), an exhortation that applies not only to an increase in the number of church members, but also (and in fact primarily) to the "edification" or growth of the church towards Christian maturity. The force of all of these passages is to remind us that *we are to work for the purity of the church.*[64]

Ministry should also show grace to the believers as part of the relationship and fellowship in and out of the church gatherings. The importance of grace is further substantiated in Acts 2:42-47, "They devoted themselves to the apostles' teaching and to fellowship, to the breaking of bread and to prayer. Everyone was filled with awe at the many wonders and signs performed by the apostles. All the believers were together and had everything in common. They sold property and possessions to give to anyone who had need. Every day they continued to meet together in the temple courts. They broke bread in their homes and ate together with glad and sincere hearts, praising God and enjoying the favor of all the people. And the Lord added to their number daily those who were being saved."

This passage shows how the early church practiced several habits such as studying the apostle's teachings, fellowship with each other, breaking bread together, praying, finding unity, meeting needs, worshipping in the temple, meeting from house to house, praising God, and having favor with all people.[65] The emphasis is that all these principles are founded in the person of Jesus Christ, who is the head of the church which is His body.

> "The glue that holds Christian churches together is Jesus Christ. When any person becomes a Christian, he or she will receive Christ into his or her heart in conversion. Conversion is not learning about a historical person, as the Buddhist learns about the historical Buddha. Conversion is not being influenced by the thoughts or sayings of a past religious leader, as Islamists revere Mohammed. Conversion is not following the example of a selfless role model who died to be an example of humility. No, conversion is none of the above. A sinner meets Christ, who is alive, because Christ was raised from the dead. Jesus sits at the right hand of God the Father in heaven. But in conversion, Christ actually enters the life believer at the moment of salvation." (Elmer Towns, *What's Right with the Church*) [66]

☙ Key Insight: We cannot reach the world if we do not equip the saints to reach their full potential.

The Evangelistic Principles

"Why would God give us a mandate that seems so impossible to accomplish? The answer is: He didn't. It is possible to reach the world with the gospel if we understand that the full development of every person is critical to reaching the world. As the person grows in Christ likeness and maturity, we intentionally create opportunities for them to engage directly in the mission of the Master. We cannot reach the world if we do not equip the saints to reach their full potential." (Rod Demsey, *Innovate Church*)[67]

The two components of the Great Commission are to evangelize and to make disciples. God gives His children the responsibility to continue the proclamation of the Gospel message.

"It is interesting to note that we are not called to stay away from the darkness. We are called to come to faith (light) and then to participate in the divine nature (2 Peter 1:4). But central to that new life is a call to go to the darkness and to bring light into the darkness. One of the fundamental definitions of a Christian is a Christ-follower. Jesus said, 'As the Father has sent me, I also send you' (John 20:21). So, we are sent like Jesus into a dark and dying world. Jesus is called the Apostle in Hebrews 3:1. An apostle is one who is sent with a message. Jesus says we are sent in the same manner. We are sent and being sent means we take the light to the darkness. In order for the lost to see the light, they must be able to understand it. This is where many people will not go. In order for the lost to understand the light, we must share our faith in ways that they can understand the light, we must share our faith in ways that they can understand. We must go to connect with them through their cultural expressions." (Elmer Towns, *Perimeters of Light*)[68]

The message must be given for professionals to understand it fully, therefore, believers in this ministry must use the means of grace, and allow God to control them by being filled by the Holy Spirit as Wayne Grudem states:

> "In Acts, there is a frequent connection between proclaiming the gospel (even in the face of opposition) and being filled with the Holy Spirit (see Acts 2:4, 14-36; 4:8; 9:17, 20; 13:9, 52). Evangelism is a means of grace, then, not only in the sense that it ministers saving grace to the unsaved, but also because those who evangelize experience more of the Holy Spirit's presence and blessing in their own lives. Sometimes evangelism is carried out by individuals, but at other times it is a corporate activity of the church (as in evangelistic campaigns). And even individual evangelism often involves other church members who will welcome an unbelieving visitor and give attention to his or her needs. So evangelism is rightly considered a means of grace in the church."[69]

Data shows the top activities or reasons given by professionals which hinder evangelism are lack of interest, career and work obligation, and family.

Table: Life Activities which Hinder to Evangelize Professionals						
	Career and Work Obligations	Family	Recreation	Lack of Interest	Belief in God	Other
Ministries	38.5%	15.4%	0.0%	46.1%	0.0%	0.0%
Professionals	20.0%	15.0%	0.0%	65.0%	0.0%	0.0%

The principles regarding the sharing of the gospel to the people of the world are found in the example of Jesus who is the Evangelist incarnate.

> "Perishing humans who come to Jesus and feel His saving grip are no longer their own. We belong to Him who holds us by His grace. And in His ownership, we participate in His mission. Evangelism thus becomes a natural expression of the church. As the body of Christ (Ephesians 4:16, 5:23, 30; Colossians

1:11, 2:19), we reflect in our individual lives that for which He gave His fleshy body on earth. To live otherwise would be a repudiation of our redeemed nature. Not to leave the issue in doubt, Jesus told His disciples that as the Father sent Him into the world, so He send us (John 17:18; 20:21). All who believe in Him now are called to His work (John 14:12). There are no exceptions. Whether we realize it or not, every Christian is a personal demonstration of the Gospel, 'known and read by all men' (2 Corinthians 3:2-3)." (Robert Coleman in his book, *The Master's Way of Personal Evangelism*) [70]

Robert Coleman lists the characteristics for believers to follow in the work of the ministry to reach professionals as exemplified by Jesus:[71]

1) Jesus became a servant to people by:
    - Going where they could find Him
    - Seeing the multitude as individuals
    - Treating people without regard to position, wealth or race
    - Responding to opportunities of ministry as they occurred
    - Utilizing the advantage of natural family relationships
    - Noticing signs of spiritual interest
    - Seeking privacy with seekers where possible
    - Taking time with people

2) Jesus inspired confidence in Himself by:
    - Showing people that He cared
    - Observing common courtesies
    - Calling people by name
    - Commending persons for their good traits
    - Asking for small favors
    - Listening to their stories
    - Interesting Himself in their interests
    - Communicating on their level

3) Jesus drew out their spiritual desire by:
    - Assuming the best

- Asking probing questions
- Stating great spiritual propositions
- Projecting the idea of God's blessings
- Illustrating His ideas
- Appealing to Scripture
- Sharing His own testimony

4) Jesus clarified the gospel by:
   - Accenting the essential truth of the kingdom
   - Uncovering sin
   - Revealing the grace of God
   - Leveling with people about the life of faith
   - Testing human motives
   - Personalizing the doctrine keeping to the subject
   - Permitting people to express their understanding of His teaching

5) Jesus brought persons to a decision by:
   - Stressing individual responsibility
   - Disclosing the alternatives
   - Challenging people to exercise faith
   - Letting people express their confidence in the most realistic way
   - Encouraging the faint hearted
   - Respecting their freedom
   - Waiting on the Spirit
   - Rejoicing in the victory

6) Jesus nurtured believers in His life by:
   - Staying with believers as time allowed
   - Explaining more about life in the Spirit
   - Stimulating witness
   - Building the Word into their lives
   - Teaching people to pray
   - Surrounding His people with a fellowship of love
   - Preparing them to face temptations in the world
   - Bringing believers into His ministry

7) Jesus expected disciples to reproduce.

☙ **Key Insight: The principles regarding the sharing of the gospel to the people of the world are found in the example of Jesus who is the Evangelist incarnate.**

The Discipleship Principles

Making disciples is the second component of the Great Commission given by Jesus. Therefore, professionals in urban metropolises reached by the ministry will be encouraged to become disciples in order to make a difference in society today.

> "What would happen for God's kingdom if we did not consider our job complete when people confess their sins and say a prayer inviting Jesus to be their Redeemer, but use their new commitment to Christ as a launching pad for a lifelong quest to become individuals who are completely sold out—emotionally, intellectually, physically, spiritually—to the Son of God?" (George Barna, *Growing the Disciples*)[72]

Data shows the top reasons professionals in metropolises do not become disciples are lack of motivation, working longer hours/overtime, and personal or family obligation as shown in the following table.

	Work Larger Hours/ Overtime Work	Public or Professionals Commitments	2nd Home or Travel	Leisure Travel	Personal or Family Obligations	Lucky Motivation
Table: Life Activities which Hinder to Disciple Professionals						
Ministers	34.6%	3.8%	0.0%	0.0%	30.8%	38.5%
Professionals	30.0%	5.0%	0.0%	0.0%	30.0%	35.0%

Barna provides six biblically based insights into discipleship which ought to be followed by professionals:[73]

1) **Disciples Must be Assured of Their Salvation by Grace Alone** (Luke 13:1-5, 20-30, 24:46-47; John 16:24-28, 20:25-28; Luke 9:1-6, 10:30-37; Acts 6:1-3; Ephesians 2:10, 4:11-12; Philippians 2:1-4; Hebrews 13:16; James 2:14-20).
2) **Disciples Must Learn and Understand the Principles of the Christian Life** (Mathew 6:33; Luke 14:25-35; Philippians 4:8-9; 2 Timothy 3:16-17; Hebrews 5:11-6:3; James 1:5).
3) **Disciples Must Obey God's Laws and Commands** (Luke 10:25-28; Acts 5:29; Galatians 5:1-24; Ephesians 4:20-5:21; Colossians 3:1-17, I Thessalonians 4:7; James 1:22-25; I John 3:16-24).
4) **Disciples Must Represent God in the World** (Mathew 10:16, 28:17-20; Mark 5:18-19; John 17:14-18; Acts 1:8; 2 Corinthians 5:20; Ephesians 4:1; Colossians 1:10; I John 2:15-17).
5) **Disciples Must Serve Other People** (Mathew 16:24-28, 20:25-28; Luke 9:1-6, 10:30-37; Acts 6:1-3; Ephesians 2:10, 4:11-12; Philippians 2:1-4; Hebrews 13:16; James 2:14-24).
6) **Disciples Must Reproduce Themselves in Christ** (Matthew 28:19; John 15:8; Matthew 9:35-38; Acts 4:1-11, 5:42, 13:47).

᠊᠊ **Key Insight: Truth becomes an entirely God-driven reality to a disciple. Pursuing the truths of God become the disciple's lifelong quest.**

Professionals who follow God's intended discipleship lifestyle will become committed, knowledgeable, practicing followers of Jesus, and instill the same capacity and motivation in others.

- Disciples experience a changed future through their acceptance of Jesus Christ as Savior and of the Christian faith as their defining philosophy of life.
- Disciples undergo a changed lifestyle that is manifested through Christ-oriented values, goals, perspectives, activities, and relationships.
- Disciples mature into a changed worldview, attributable to a deeper comprehension of the true meaning and impact of

Christianity. Truth becomes entirely God-driven reality to a disciple. Pursuing the truths of God becomes the disciple's lifelong quest. (Barna, *Growing the Disciples*)[74]

The discipleship process is a path for spiritual growth in which biblically based practices or spiritually disciplines will be taught and put in practice by professionals.

"We must not be led to believe that the Disciplines are only for spiritual giants and hence beyond our reach, or only for contemplatives who devote all their time to prayer and meditation. Far from it, God intends the Disciplines of the spiritual life to be for ordinary human beings: people who have jobs, who care for children, who wash dishes and mow lawns. In fact, the Disciplines are best exercised in the midst of our relationships with our husband or wife, our brothers and sisters, our friends and neighbors." (Richard Foster, *Celebration of Disciple*)[75]

The Three Categories of Spiritual Disciplines:[76]

The Inward Disciplines:[77]

- Meditation–to learn to hear God's voice and obey His word
- Prayer–to transform by bringing us closer to the heartbeat of God
- Fasting–abstaining from food for spiritual purposes
- Study–to enable the mind to move in a biblical direction

The Outward Disciplines:[78]

- Simplicity–an inward reality that results in an outward life-style
- Solitude–a state of mind and heart to focus in the will of God
- Submission–an inner attitude of mutual subordination
- Service–not through human effort, not impressed with the "big deal," doesn't require external rewards, doesn't pick whom to serve, not affected by moods and whims, is not insensitive

The Corporate Disciplines:[79]

- Confession–open and accountable according to the will of God
- Worship–response to love from the heart of the Father
- Guidance–leading in accordance with the will of God
- Celebration–a joyful spirit of contentment with thankfulness towards what God is doing in the believer's life.

The Ministry to Reach Professional Principles

The ministry goal is to grow by following God's principles given in the Bible and reproduce with accountability, sharing of resources (stewardship), infusion of trained workers shared vision and core values, greater prayer support, pre-established network for problem solving, and not reinventing the wheel through connection with others doing the same thing.[80]

> "The church is in serious decline, perhaps unlike any time in America's past. Not only vast numbers of people unchurched, but a number of Christians are dropping out of church. And many of these are spiritually vibrant people who feel that their church experience is doing them and their families more harm than good. I believe new model-churches could offer a viable answer to this dilemma." (Audry Malphurs, *A New Kind of Church*)[81]

People think different today. A person's faith is no longer tied to the church or its ministry, and weekly gathering such as on Sunday morning is no longer valued.[82] The professionals' ministry must address the lack of interest and other activities in the life of the professionals and their families that hinder evangelizing and discipling them. Therefore, the ministry must share the essentials of the faith and adapt the nonessentials to the specific needs and direction without affecting the Great Commission.

The Five Essentials:

1. The Bible is the inspired Word of God.
2. There is only one true God as three coequal and coeternal persons (the Trinity).
3. The deity and substitutionary atonement of Christ provide for salvation by faith apart from baptism or works.
4. Christ was bodily resurrected.
5. Christ will physically return to earth (Ephesians 4:3-16).[83]

Dealing with the Nonessentials:

1. *Church Government (policy)*. Policy addresses where the power should be in the church and who makes the major decisions that impact the church.
2. *Mode of Baptism*. Most who baptize believe in immersion, sprinkling, or pouring.
3. *The Lord's Supper*. Whether or not the elements convey grace to the recipients.
4. *Role of Women in the Church*. Full participation including ordination and the senior pastor's office, little or no participation.
5. *Spiritual Gifts*. Belief that only some gifts or all the gifts are for today.
6. *When the Church Meets*. Sunday morning or night, or any day is permissible.
7. *Church Practices*. Serve communion and/or teach the Scriptures every meeting.[84]

The Core Values:

1. Evangelism theology of aggressive outreach
2. Strong pastoral leadership
3. Participatory worship
4. Powerful prayer
5. Centrality of the Holy Spirit
6. Abundant finances through tithing

7. Lay ministry
8. Practical Bible teaching
9. Direct missions involvement
10. Low denominational profile.[85]

Only professionals who deal with the day to day challenges associated with their personal and work life, and who have found purpose in Christ, will be able to lead other professionals with words of encouragement, exhortation/wise counsel, and giving to assist the material needs of a brother or sister.

The Professional's Pursuit of the Presence of God

There is no doubt that professionals struggle with sin, although they might not see some of their actions as sinful due to the current society trend where many of the sins listed in the following table are widely approved in the metropolises lifestyle (see Galatians 5:19-21).

Table: Professionals Struggle with Sins						
	Ministers			Professionals		
Sin	Yes	No	Don't Know	Yes	No	Don't Know
Immorality	100.0%	0.0%	0.0%	60.0%	5.0%	35.0%
Impurity	90.0%	10.0%	0.0%	60.0%	0.0%	40.0%
Sensuality	100.0%	0.0%	0.0%	60.0%	0.0%	40.0%
Idolatry	90.0%	0.0%	10.0%	60.0%	0.0%	40.0%
Drunkenness	100.0%	0.0%	0.0%	20.0%	15.0%	65.0%
Sorcery	70.0%	20.0%	10.0%	5.0%	55.0%	40.0%
Coursing	80.0%	10.0%	10.0%	40.0%	0.0%	60.0%
Enmities	90.0%	10.0%	0.0%	50.0%	0.0%	50.0%
Strife	90.0%	0.0%	10.0%	60.0%	0.0%	40.0%
Envy	100.0%	0.0%	0.0%	60.0%	0.0%	40.0%
Jealousy	90.0%	0.0%	10.0%	60.0%	0.0%	40.0%
Outburst Anger	80.0%	10.0%	10.0%	60.0%	0.0%	40.0%
Disputes	90.0%	0.0%	10.0%	60.0%	0.0%	40.0%
Dissension	90.0%	0.0%	10.0%	60.0%	0.0%	40.0%
Factions	90.0%	0.0%	10.0%	60.0%	0.0%	40.0%

This author took a walk through the Bible in order to find principles of what God expects from Christians in order to follow the call to pursue His presence every day of their lives as shown in Chart or Table.

Table: The Call to Pursue the Presence of God	
Scripture	**What the Call is...**
Romans 12:1-2	The urgency to follow the will of God
2 Corinthians 5:11	to live in peace
Galatians 2:20-21	to live in Christ
Galatians 5:16-26	to live and walk by the Spirit
Ephesians 4:20-32	to live in the likeness of God
Ephesians 6:10-24	to use the armor of God in order to fight our spiritual warfare against the enemy
Philippians 2:1-4	to have the mind of Christ
Philippians 4:4-8	to have the thoughts of Christ
Ephesians 5:15-17	to understand the will of God and use our time wisely
Colossians 3:10-17	to put on the new self with the peace and word of Christ
1 Timothy 6:6-19	to live a godly life with contentment
2 Timothy 2:15-17	to handle the word of truth accurately
Hebrews 11:6	to have faith in order to please God
Hebrews 12:14	to pursue peace with all men
James 2:14-26	to show faith by works
1 John 2:15-17	not to love the world nor the things of the world
Revelation 22:7	not to forget His second coming and understood eternal life in His presence

The Professionals' ministry should promote pursuing the presence of God in order to understand their specific life path of service to God. Professionals must know God and understand, that sooner or later they will cross over the line beyond this life into eternity, thus the only relationship which will matter is the one with God. The above table is a guideline of basic principles that should be introduced early and reinforced often in a professional ministry to help promote the presence of God in each individual's life. The stronger the understanding of God's calling by an individual, the more likely they are to apply the principles in their daily life, even without regular "church" attendance.

> **Key Insight: Understanding of God as completely sovereign, infinite in wisdom, and perfect in love will keep their focus in the overall purpose of their lives.**

J. I. Packer's Four Evidences of Knowing God:

1. Those who know God have great energy for God. People who know their God are before anything else people who pray. Their zeal and energy for God's glory is expressed in their prayers.
2. Those who know God have great thoughts for God.
3. Those who know God show great boldness for God. They find seeking the right course is agonizingly difficult, but once they are clear on it they embrace it boldly and without hesitation. It does not worry them that others of God's people see the matter differently and do not stand with them.
4. Those who know God have great contentment in God. There is no peace like the peace of those who know God, and know God knows them, and that this relationship guarantees God's favor to them in life, through death and on to forever.[86]

Furthermore, Packer says that the pursuit of God is essential for each believer as he states, "The Lord Jesus Christ is now absent from us in body, but spiritually it makes no difference; still we may find and know God through seeking and findings Jesus' company. It is those who have sought the Lord Jesus till have they have found him–for the promise is that when we seek with all our hearts we shall surely find him–who can stand before the world to testify that they have known God."[87]

✓**Action Challenge: The professionals' ministry should promote pursuing the presence of God in their lives in order to understand their specific life path of service to God.**

This pursuit to know God is vital in the ministry to reach professionals as Packer writes, "But for all this, we must not lose sight of the fact that knowing God is an emotional relationship, as well an intellectual and volitional one, and could not indeed be a deep relation between persons were it not so. The believer is and must be, emotionally involved in the victories and vicissitudes of God's cause in the world."[88]

The pursuit of the practice of knowing God and His presence is to help those who follow to attain "Christian perfection"[89] and preservation from sin. John MacArthur states, "the first foundation pillar God's people must have is spiritual faith, a trust in God. And that attitude will not grow and develop unless individual believers come to know God better and better."[90]

As professionals pursue the presence of God, they will experience growing their faith, trusting in God, and pursuing holiness. Therefore, when adversity comes their way, the understanding of God as completely sovereign, infinite in wisdom, and perfect in love will keep their focus in the overall purpose of their lives. Christians will see in due time the fruit of the Spirit in their lives when they experience their faith and trust in God to grow.

Regarding holiness, which is vital in the process of knowing God, Jerry Bridges shares, "The holiness of God is an exceedingly high standard, a perfect standard: But it is nevertheless one that He holds us to. He cannot do less. While it is true that He accepts us solely through the merit of Christ, God's standard for our character, attitudes, affections and actions is, 'Be holy, because, I am holy.' We must take this seriously if we are to grow in holiness."[91]

Take the time to review the key insights gleaned from this chapter and begin to put them into practice in your own life.

⚿ Key Insights from Chapter

Christianity is not about rules though it does have principles. It's about Jesus Christ.

We cannot reach the world if we do not equip the saints to reach their full potential.

The principles regarding sharing the gospel to the people of the world are found in the example of Jesus who is the Evangelist incarnate.

Truth becomes entirely God-driven reality to a disciple. Pursuing the truths of God become the disciple's lifelong quest.

Understanding of God as completely sovereign, infinite in wisdom, and perfect in love will keep their focus on the overall purpose of their lives.

✓ Action Challenges from Chapter 4

The professionals' ministry should promote pursuing the presence of God in their lives in order to understand their specific life path of service to God.

- *Will the ministry effectively disciple professionals?*
- *Do the ministry methods line up with the Great Commission?*
- *Will the ministry gatherings involve people ministering to each other?*
- *Will the ministry equip in the pursuit of the presence of God relative to modern day circumstances in a practical way?*

Chapter 5

Practical Implications to Reach Professionals

Therefore, I urge you, brethren by the mercies of God, to present your bodies a living and holy sacrifice, acceptable to God, which is your spiritual service of worship. And do not be conformed to this world, but be transformed by the renewing of your mind, so that you may prove what the will of God is, that is good and acceptable and perfect. (Romans 12:1-2)

God, in His sovereign will, has allowed humanity to change and move into new cultural, social, technology, and other trends with the passing of time. Today, we are dealing with a new society environment in the metropolises where professionals live. The Great Commission must be carried out with methods based on the Bible and the principles it states to live for God. Based on the findings of this work, along with my life experiences as a consulting engineer professional for over three decades, methods to evangelize and disciple professionals for this time in our history are considered in this chapter.

The Church Methods

The ministry to reach professionals will team with local church congregations in the metropolises where it is based. This partnership in the Body of Christ serves two purposes. The first being that the Professional's Ministry will have a local church to which they are able to refer new believers as the believers need services and support beyond what the Professional's Ministry can provide. Secondly, it promotes a partnership and unity among believers that provides a positive example and could influence the views of professionals towards the "corporate church." The ministry will run independently from church congregations and other ministries from an administrative and operational standpoint. This is so as not to overburden churches already facing challenges supporting existing ministries. By keeping the ministry separate, it may also promote attendance by professionals who, at the current time, have no interest in attending a traditional church. This ministry will be similar to Campus Crusade for Christ, Focus on the Family, and others which follow this interdependent approach with churches and ministries as a team in reaching those who do not know Christ as personal Lord and Savior. The following diagram shows a cooperation model between the professionals and other ministries in the Southeast Florida metropolses.

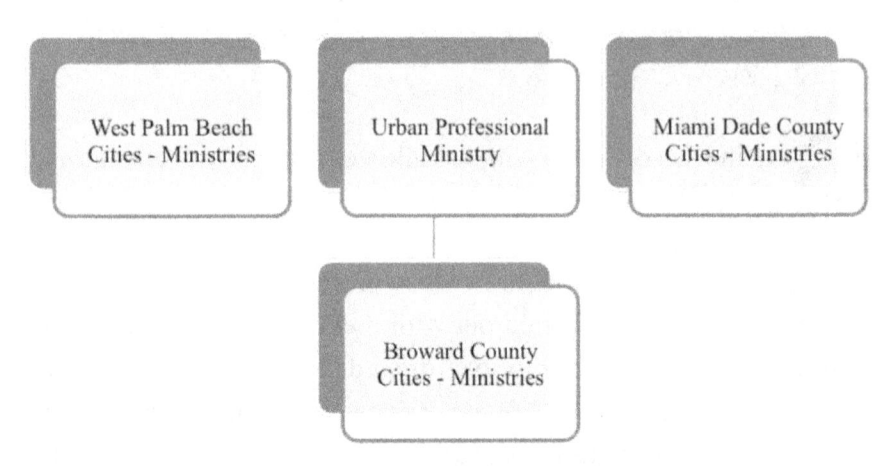

```
┌─────────────────┐   ┌─────────────────┐   ┌─────────────────┐
│ West Palm Beach │   │ Urban Professional│  │ Miami Dade County│
│ Cities - Ministries│ │    Ministry     │   │ Cities - Ministries│
└─────────────────┘   └────────┬────────┘   └─────────────────┘
                               │
                      ┌─────────────────┐
                      │ Broward County  │
                      │ Cities - Ministries│
                      └─────────────────┘
```

Diagram: Metropolises Ministries and Churches
Cooperation with the Professional Ministry

Elmer Towns writes, "The North American's church is not on a mission field. Over the last few decades, the church in North America has lost the home-field advantage. Today, we are living in a jungle of lostness, not a religious society that looks to us for leadership. Pastors are being attacked and crippled for ministry. Some are driven out of ministry altogether. The reputation of God is being 'dragged through the mud.' The glory of God is adequate with pulpit or healing sensationalism. Evangelism is equated with being non-offensive, non-confrontational, or tolerant of other religious ways of 'salvation.' Lost people are often hostile to the gospel and the issue has to be addressed."[92]

The churches and other ministries in metropolises will have the Professionals' Ministry as an extension in the mission field to reach professional groups on a one-to-one or small group setting, as the most effective gathering methods to reach them.

In his book, *Perimeters of Light,* Elmer Towns provides additional insight regarding this church approach of working with methods to bring the message to the professionals to be reached in one-to-one or small group gatherings.

> "Today the American church is under attack. It's trying desperately to hold on to the territory previously 'won' from the darkness. But, some of its light-bearers flirt with the darkness. Some in the emerging church are making the same mistake that countless other groups have. Can the darkness teach us how to make fire? Can the night enlighten others? Can the world show us how to evangelize? To live holy lives? Obviously, we would answer 'no' to all these questions, and rightly so. Yet, our task is not just the rejection of culture; we must also take the light to each setting."[93]

The professionals' ministry will collaborate with the local churches in order to bridge the professionals reached by the ministry into their congregations. The ministry will carefully evaluate each professional's current life circumstances and ministry needs, and will suggest local churches or ministries where he or she can join and gather when the professionals are called to delve deeper in their walk with Christ and the local Christian community. The local churches are already equipped with ministries to children, youth, college, career, young adults, families, seniors, special need populations, and many others beyond the scope of the urban professionals' ministry focus of work. This approach to help professionals receive ministry based on current life needs is a contemporary example of how the Body of Christ can work as a team in order to carry out the Great Commission. There has been an unfortunate tendency by many in ministry to use a "solo approach" which leads to a selfish and un-biblically-based purpose. Promoting "church exclusivity" or an "all or nothing" involvement is a worldly approach reminiscent of the high school social scene and not biblically sound. Christ teaches we are one body, working together, for His purpose. By not working together with a team mindset for the glory of God, many professionals and other evangelized groups have "slipped through the cracks."

This team approach requires keeping a spiritual focus on prayer, the big picture, and God. It also requires keeping the vision alive, sharing the vision, winning people to the vision, nurturing the vision, helping people to claim the vision, working with those who support the vision, adjusting the needs of the church-ministry team, and making the right choices.[94] The relationship between the ministry and the congregations requires a series of practical attitudes to ensure succes.

> **Key Insight: By not working together with a team mindset with other ministries for the glory of God, many professionals and other evangelized groups have "slipped through the cracks."**

Peter Scazzero in his book, *The Emotionally Healthy Church*, presents qualities the leaders working this team effort ought to possess:

1) Transparency
2) An awareness of his or her own limitations and freedom to admit failure

3) Approachable and open to input
4) Aware of his own brokenness and slow to judge others
5) Slow to speak and quick to listen
6) Care about others
7) Understands their own limitations so that Christ's power may be seen
8) Willing to give people an opportunity to earn his or her trust
9) Understand that God's strength reveals itself in admitting mistakes, weakness, and saying, "I was wrong."
10) Take responsibility for his or her own actions
11) Forgiving
12) When offended, ask questions to explore what happened
13) Looks at the truth underneath the surface even when it hurts
14) Be present with people in their pain, and comfortable with misery. Say, "I don't know" instead of trying to fabricate excuses or reasons
15) Let things go
16) Assert respectfully and kindly
17) More aware of God and others than the impression being made by himself
18) See people as gifts to be loved and enjoyed.[95]

If the leaders in the Urban Professionals Ministries and the local churches can incorporate the above traits in the partnership with each other, and in the manner in which they reach professionals, the current misconceptions of the Church held by professionals will slowly begin to fade and hearts, previously lost, will be won for Christ.

The Evangelistic Methods

Professionals will be invited, by word of mouth and other conventional advertisement methods(social media, printed flyers in public locations, targeted calendar announcements in professional group e-mails and publications), to a once a month evangelistic session by this ministry to be held in a social club, hotel ballroom or similar location in the metropolis where the ministry resides. The gospel of Christ will be presented along with a practical and contemporary topic presentation which affects the life of these professionals. This gathering method will be complemented by one-on-one and other small or large group gatherings where the opportunity to present the gospel will be given. The intent is to get people into the body of Christ.

Elmer Towns' book, *Perimeters of Light,* says:

1) The success of the church does not depend on a continuation of a modernity culture, but on the creation of a New Testament church that reflects the new culture.
2) Because Jesus Christ is with us (Matthew 28:20), we do not have to fear a new set of methods, or paradigms; but rather we must focus on the power of Jesus Christ and His gospel, which will be our new set of rules and paradigms.
3) Our challenge is not continue our traditions or a culture from modernity, or to create new customs for postmodern, but rather we must "immerse" every new believer into a community of like-faith believers from his or her culture, and then give each believer the commission to reach others in that culture.
4) Being a disciple means more than knowing the facts of Christianity; it also involves following Jesus Christ so that his or her Christianity is involved in experiences, relationships, learning, and serving.
5) To evangelize by making disciples is both a decision and a process. This means we must acknowledge that individuals are at different levels of understanding, feeling, and readiness to respond to the gospel. We must understand that following Jesus Christ is a *decision* when the person chooses to follow Jesus Christ, and then it becomes a *process* as the person continues to follow Jesus Christ.
6) The challenge is to evangelize every person in every culture so that he or she believes in Jesus Christ. Then, each one must "acculturate" Christ into his/her life and thinking, which involves making disciples within each ethnic group. We will not change the church into the expectations of the postmodern, but we can aim to transform the postmodern into the image of Jesus Christ. Many in a postmodern age

may start further away from Christ than their predecessors in a once nominally Christian America. It may take them longer to be assimilated into a culturally Christian church in America; they can be assimilated more quickly into their ethnic church that has "acculturated" Jesus Christ.[96] But a mixer is familiar for urban professionals, and combining Christ's teachings in a setting that most see as non-threatening, requiring minimal commitment at just once a month, and surrounded by their peers may be just enough modification to encourage professionals to return to Christ.

☛ Key Insight: The challenge is to evangelize every person in every culture so that he or she believes in Jesus Christ.

Luke provides the narrative in Acts 24:1-26:32 about Paul's experiences when witnessing before Gentiles and the Jewish King. Paul appeared before Governor Felix (Acts 24), Governor Festus (25:1-22), and the titular Jewish King Agrippa II (Acts 25:23- 26-32) to present his defense against the Jewish charges with the end result of witnessing about Christ and His resurrection.

Three accusations were made against Paul (Acts 24:5-8):

1) He was a worldwide trouble maker, stirring up riots everywhere.
2) He was a leader of the Nazarene sect.
3) He attempted to desecrate the temple.

To these accusations Paul gave several points in his own defense. First, he had not been in Jerusalem long enough to instigate a riot, but his purpose was to worship God. Second, Paul's attackers could not indicate instances of him instigating riots in the city. Third, Paul worshipped the God of Israel in full conformity with the Law and Prophets.

Luke presents Paul as a respectful and non-imposing individual who simply stated the facts about Christ, and used the circumstances available for him to give the gospel message. Professionals in general can be open to dialogue on a subject about God or religion if they approach the conversation with an open mind on the beliefs of others even if they do not agree. Therefore, agreeing to disagree is a common ground to have conversations between professionals about topics that can become controversial between individuals.

Some of the results found in Paul's witnessing experience with Felix, Festus, and Agrippa are summarized from the *Book of Acts* by John B. Polhill:

> "Witness to Felix: He demonstrated a genuine concern to hear the apostle's testimony. His alarm at Paul's message was real. Felix did not dismiss Paul's reference to the judgment as fantasy. He appeared fearful but never was willing to go beyond the point and take the leap of faith since at the end, his greed; lust and desire to preserve his power carried the day."[97]

> "Witness to Festus: He seemed to imply that Paul was himself responsible for the whole situation with the unnecessary appeal, but he acknowledges Paul's innocence."[98]

> "Witness to Agrippa II and Festus: Paul gave what is considered the most elevated and cultural language speeches in Acts. This speech is parallel to the one Paul gave to the temple mob. In both occasions, Paul gave a testimony of his personal experience in Christ, Jewish upbringing, persecution of the Christians, conversion and commission from the risen Lord. Paul concluded preaching to the Agrippa and Gentiles gathered by sharing forgiveness of sins, which is the removal of the barrier that separates one from God, and the assurance of a place among the saints in God's eternal Kingdom. Furthermore, Paul gave an object lesson in bold witness at this point while addressing Agrippa. At the end, Paul was declared innocent by Festus and Agrippa, thus, still he was on his way to Rome in chains."[99]

The evangelistic efforts must emphasize the perimeters of Christianity belief and ministry:

1) Jesus

2) The Gospel
3) Bible Doctrine
4) Christian Experience
5) God's Blessing.[100]

In addition, the following biblical teachings must be taken into account when sharing the gospel message with professionals:

1) The authority and perfection of Scripture as the revelation of God's person and will. Take away the authority of the Bible, or the essential content of the Bible, and you no longer have Christianity.
2) The deity of Jesus Christ. God who was born of a virgin to become fully man, and man who is fully God. Take away the truth of His virgin birth and you no longer have Christianity.
3) The substitutionary atonement of Jesus Christ for sins, displayed in the shedding of His blood. If forgiveness of sins by the blood is missing from the message, it is not the Christian message.
4) The physical resurrection of Jesus Christ from death to give us new life.
5) The bodily return of Jesus Christ to take His children to live with Him and to judge those who reject His plan of salvation.[101]

Focusing on just the basics will help reach professionals, even with just a single monthly meeting, by stripping away anything unnecessary and expressly conveying the basic principles of Christianity. This supports the creation of a strong foundation on which a solid relationship with Christ is formed.

The Discipleship Methods

The ministry goal after reaching professionals in the evangelistic effort and having them make a profession of faith is to make them disciples of Christ. This discipleship process will either take place in the ministry setting with its resources or in another church congregation where the new believers might want to attend due to specific ministry needs for them and their families.

⁌ Key Insight: The ministry goal is to make them disciples of Christ.

George Barna in his book, *Growing True Disciples,* describes the true discipleship characteristics which this ministry will promote among those who become believers:
- True discipleship produces holistic personal transformation, not mere assimilation into a community of church members.
- True discipleship is witnessed by people who are determined to be a blessing to others-people who are never content to simply accept and enjoy God's blessings.
- True discipleship creates Christians who aggressively pursue spiritual growth rather than passively experience spiritual evolution.
- True discipleship spawns individuals who develop renewed lifestyles instead of believers who mechanically check off completed assignments on a developmental agenda.
- True discipleship results in people who are more concerned about the quality of their character than the extent of their knowledge.
- True discipleship builds churches known for their culture of love, commitment, and service rather than for their events, information, and programs.
- True discipleship facilitates people devoted to a lifelong journey to imitate Jesus Christ rather than the completion of a short-term regimen of tasks and responsibilities.[102]

The data from the research findings show how clergy and professionals concur about the importance of using Bible studies and home setting gatherings to disciple professionals, thus making the development of local chapters of a Professional's Ministry a logical and beneficial next step in evangelizing the American working professional.

Practical Implications to Reach Professionals

Table: Methods to Encourage Professionals to be Disciples						
	Adult Sunday School	Bible Study	Special Conferences	Retreats	Sports	Attendance to Cultural of Sports Events
Ministers	30.7%	53.8	11.5%	3.8%	0.0%	.0.0%
Professionals	0.0%	60.0%	10.0%	30.0%	0.0%	0.0%

☛ **Key Insight: "The real obstacles to becoming fully devoted zealous disciples of Christ are not money, time, methods or knowledge. The major obstacle is the human heart."[103]**

Acts 17:16-34 discusses Paul's experience in Athens when he witnessed to the center of Gentile culture and intellect. He spoke to the Epicurean and Stoic philosophers in a speech for which the main theme was God as Creator and the proper worship of this Creator God. The language he used often had the ring of Greek philosophy for Paul was attempting to build what bridges he could by using a manner of speaking familiar to them, to reach the Athenian intellectuals while remaining thoroughly biblical.

Paul received three responses from the audience concerning his speech. The first response was related to the Epicureans' belief there is no human existence after death. The Stoics' believed that only the immaterial spirit survived death. Therefore, the Greek idea of a body surviving death did not make sense, thus, many scoffed at Paul's reference to the resurrection. Others wanted to hear him again; and a few, including Dionysius the Areopagite and Damaris responded in faith.[104] This simple evangelism technique – using language and communication methods tailored to those you are trying to reach – provided Paul with greater results than had he not changed his method of delivery. It is very important to note that Paul **did not change the message** and was still able to bring new believers to Christ among Greek academics.

The data from the research findings shows how both clergy and professionals do not see academics, financial resources, and influence in the community as greatly affecting professionals to become faithful followers of Christ. Interpreting these findings, it is evident that the message used to minister to professionals should be no different than the message used to minister to anyone else. Despite potentially different social standing, education, and financial resources, the need for Christ is present as it is for all humans. The goal now for clergy is to reach professionals using a method they understand, that will engage them in a conversation and a life-changing thought process to bring them to Christ.

Table: Professional Life Characteristics Helping to Become a Faithful Follower of Christ						
		Academics	Financial Resources	Influence in the Community	Others
Ministers	Yes	15.3%	7.7%	19.2%	N/A
	No	84.6%	92.3%	80.8%	N/A
Professionals	Yes	35.0%	15.0%	20.0%	N/A
	No	65.0%	85.0%	80.0%	N/A

The Ministry to Reach Professionals–Methods

The ministry methods to reach professionals will have the goal to follow the Great Commission, start a revolution for God in this first quarter of the 21st Century, so as to experience what Elmer Towns defines as a revival.

> "An extraordinary work of God in which Christians repent of their sins as they become intensely aware of His presence in their midst and manifest a positive response to God in renewal obedience to the known will of God, resulting in both a deepening in their individual and corporate experience with God and increased concern for the spiritual welfare of both themselves and others within their community."[105]

The ministry will create an environment with biblical conditions to inspire an outpouring of the Holy Spirit in ways such as:

- A desire for revival
- Interventional prayer for revival
- Repentance of known sin
- Yielding to the Lordship of Christ
- Unity of fellowship
- Praise and worship of God
- Giving to God[106]

These conditions, along with a leadership in the ministry which is committed to the cause of Christ, help create an operational structure to make disciples in accordance with the Great Commission mandate. This ministry will reach professionals once a month with evangelistic and discipleship gatherings in which the program content will consist of topics that can help professionals in their individual relationships with family, fellow workers in their workplaces, and others based on the teachings from the Bible. This includes personally knowing and having the tools to effectively communicate spiritual theology, the story of God's perfect community, and God's perfect plan. Larry Crabb expresses these same thoughts in his book, *Real Church,* where he writes:

> "I want to be part of a gathering of Christians, few or many, who learn spiritual theology, long for spiritual formation, pay the price to develop spiritual community, and give themselves to spiritual missions; a group of believers who feel unbearable pity for the suffering of mankind and realize they can do something about it as they wait for Jesus to return and bring His perfect plan to fruition in perfect community, so that His Father, for the first time, can look at His people and His world and say, 'This is good it's very, very, good!' That's a *real church!*"[107]

The people who are redeemed will be encouraged to follow God's will in their lives, not out of a social obligation, but from a genuine personal revival experienced through starting, or renewing, a relationship with Christ via the ministry. Based on specific individual circumstances, guidance will be provided to professionals to join a specific local church congregation or ministry partner for their care and fellowship.

Chuck Swindoll offers pertinent advice for those carrying out such ministry:

1) **Think spiritually!** Clear, biblical thinking must override secular planning and a corporate mentality.
2) **Stay biblical!** Studied, accurate decisions must originate from God's Word, not human opinions.
3) **Be flexible!** Wise, essential changes must occur to counteract any sign of erosion.[108]

✓**Action Challenge: "Unless there is ample training for facilitators, a tight accountability process, strong relational connections, and a purposeful selection of material to cover, the small groups will fail to produce disciples."[109]**

The discipleship process for this ministry to reach professionals will consider the advice by George Barna in his book, *Growing True Disciples,* where he writes:

- ☐ Recognize that disciple making is a process, not a program.
- ☐ The process will not occur without leadership from the senior leadership.
- ☐ The church's ministry focus must be streamline to prioritize and support discipleship.
- ☐ The process is not likely to succeed unless there is a simple but intelligent plan for growth.
- ☐ The process will not generate true disciples unless it has a designated supervisor to facilitate progress, faster creative problem solving and development, and strive for reasonable outcomes.
- ☐ In creating a process that works, adapt lessons learned from other churches to your own ministry context.

Practical Implications to Reach Professionals

- ☐ Be prepared for burnout and complacency to set in after two or three years on involvement in the intensive process.
- ☐ Carefully balance the completion interest of flexibility and structure.
- ☐ Keep your eyes on one goal: We are dedicated to producing genuine followers of Jesus Christ. That demands that we help people develop a biblical worldview and a compassionate heart. Highly effective disciple-making churches dwell on how they can direct peoples' minds, hearts, and energy toward being devoted to a transformed life. They are not perfect churches, and do not have perfect disciples. But they're getting closer to those outcomes day by day, by virtue of their clearly articulated, single minded devotion to growing true disciples.[110]

Research data shows how professionals who are redeemed in Christ might pursue involvement in the ministry if properly led within the understanding of his or her current circumstances.

Table: Activities Professionals want to Pursue in Church Ministries						
		Activity A	Activity B	Activity C	Activity D	Activity E
Ministers	Yes	84.6%	65.4%	73.1%	61.5%	57.7%
	No	15.4%	34.6%	26.9%	38.5%	62.3%
Professionals	Yes	80.0%	60.0%	75.0%	50.0%	50.0%
	No	20.0%	40.0%	25.0%	50.0%	50.0%

Table activities description are as follows:

A: Read and Study the Bible
B: Sacrifice for a specific purpose for the Kingdom
C: Pray for the entire world for the will of God to be done
D: Spend time in the work of evangelism and discipleship
E: Commit to multiply the church congregation community

To accomplish this requires the development of leaders that focus on strengths, develop the top 20 percent in the ministry, treat the leaders as individuals for impact, give power away, invest time in others, grow by multiplication, and desire to impact people beyond their own reach.

Practical Methods for the Pursuit of the Presence of God

Everybody dies, with the exception of Enoch and Elijah who were taken to Heaven. This day to day evidence about the shortness of life should encourage humans in the pursuit of who God is, and what takes place after one crosses over the line of being alive on this earth to eternity. Therefore, the ministry will promote the goal of knowing God.

John Piper in his book, *Desiring God,* states,

> Jesus Christ is coming back not only to effect the final salvation of His people, but through His salvation "to be glorified in his saints, and to be marveled at among all who have believed." A final comment concerns history's climax in the book of Revelation: John pictures the New Jerusalem, the glorified church 21:23: "The city has no need of sun or moon to shine on it, for the glory of God gives it light, and its lamp is the Lamb." God the Father and God the Son are the light in which Christians will live there eternity. This is the consummation of God's goal in all of history – to display His glory for all to see and praise. The prayer of the Son confirms the final purpose of the Father: Father, I desire that they also, whom you have given me, may be with me where I am, *to see my glory*, that you have given me because you loved me before the foundation of the world" (John 17:24). What may we conclude from this survey of redemptive history? We may conclude that the chief end of God is to glorify God and enjoy Himself forever. He stands supreme at the center of His own affections. For that very reason, He is a self-sufficient and inexhaustible fountain of grace.[111]

Professionals attending the ministry gathering will be encouraged to trust God, acknowledge His sovereignty and His goodness, learn from the Scriptures that God is in control of their lives, that He loves them, and works at all the circumstances of their lives for their ultimate good.[112] The intent is to help them develop an intimate walk with God in which they know Him on a personal basis, and understand the individual and special call and purpose for which God made them.

Jerry Bridges provides guidance on how to mature in Christ in his book, *Growing Your Faith,* where he shares his thoughts on the marks of spiritual growth:

1) Growing in Christian character. This will grow the motivation to obey God out of a sense of gratitude and reverence to Him. It is important to note that obedience will always be imperfect in performance in this life, and motives will never be consistently pure; there will be frequently some "merit points" mentally mixed with our one's genuine love and reverence for God.[113]
2) The Pursuit of Holiness. God calls Hid children to be holy or to separate themselves from sin.[114]
3) The Practice of Godliness. This is the personal attitude towards God that results in actions that are pleasing God. This means to show faith by works. [115]
4) Serving God. He created people with gifts, natural abilities, and temperament to be used in His purposes. [116]
5) Worshipping God. This is done individually and corporately with other believers.[117]

George Barna in his book, *Maximum Faith,* outlines ten stops on our journey toward maturity in Christ:

1) Ignorance of the concept or existence of sin
2) Awareness of an indifferent to sin
3) Concern about the implications of personal sin
4) Confession of sins and asking Jesus Christ to be their Savior
5) Commitment to faith activities

6) Experience a prolonged period of spiritual discontent
7) Experience personal brokenness
8) Choosing to surrender and submit fully to God: radical dependence
9) Enjoy profound intimacy with and love for God
10) Experience a profound compassion and love for humanity.[118]

The above findings by Barna are a method to monitor the stage stops in the life process of professionals.

Research findings indicate that 100 percent of the clergy surveyed concur that the practice of the spiritual disciplines of prayer, mediation, fasting, and studying the Word will help professionals in the pursuit of the presence of God.

Table: Activities for Professionals to Pursue the Presence of God						
		Prayer	**Meditation**	**Fasting**	**Studying the Word**	**Others**
Ministers	Yes	100.0%	100.0%	100.0%	100.0%	N/A
	No	0.0%	0.0%	0.0%	0.0%	N/A
Professionals	Yes	100.0%	85.0%	75.0%	95.0%	N/A
	No	0.0%	15.0%	25.0%	5.0%	N/A

This ministry will promote a life of faith as described by Elmer Towns in his book, *Big Bold Extraordinary Faith,* when he says:

"Living by faith includes so much more than trusting in God for money. *Living by faith* does include trusting God for money, so all pastors and all lay people must trust God daily for daily bread. But in the final analysis, *living by faith* includes much more than money; it touches every part of your life. You must live your whole life by all the principles found in God's Word. And those who do, will have the greater foundation to live by faith. When you live by faith, you'll live every day, in every way, by the principles of God."[119]

This faith will be promoted by studying the Word of God, practicing prayer and obedience to God, exercising godliness and good works, seeking God, seeking constant cleansing by the blood of Christ, yielding to God's will, communion with God, gratitude to

God, and not trusting in self. This list may not say everything a person must do to grow his faith, but it is a good place to start.[120]

Professionals reached by the ministry will be taught to have proper life perspectives as presented by Richard Swenson in his book, *Margin,* when he shares:

In his influential writings, Wilberforce makes several references to the importance of progress. Yet it is not progress in wealth, education, and power that he speaks of, but instead, progress in virtue. This, he suggest, could be measured by "this fear and love of God and of Christ; love, kindness, and meekness toward our fellow men; indifference to the possessions and events of this life compared with our concern about eternity; self-denial and humility. It does not sound much like our current definition of progress, but it does sound hopeful. Discerning Christians have long known that God is not impressed with our wealth, education, or power. Nevertheless, we have labored eagerly in those fields. What if, instead we were to begin measuring our progress not by our wealth but our virtue; not by our education but by 3our humility; and not by our power but by our meekness? Graduate degrees and GNPs will never usher in the kingdom – only love can do that. And love brings us back to Wilberforce: "Above all, measure your progress by your experience of the love God and its exercise before men.[121]

> **⁊ Key Insight: There are two rules to consider regarding contentment to relate correctly to money and in a similar way to possessions: 1) God comes first and possessions come second and 2) possessions are to be used, not loved.**[122]

Following these rules will help anyone live with simplicity and avoid the pitfalls described by Richard Swenson:

1) Society's disrespect. If we choose to ignore fashion and status, we will not gain the admiration of our peers.
2) Our own expectations. Gratification of our appetites has become a widespread goal not seriously challenged by the Church.

3) Our lack of discipline. We have not needed many disciplines during this era of abundance, we have lost interest in abundance, and we have lost interest in it as a component of lifestyle.
4) Our own mistaken opinions. Theological confusion has permitted us to look at what we want and then to build a theology that justifies it. Instead, we need to judge our opinions repeatedly with the truth of Scriptures.[123]

The ministry will help professionals live a life with purpose in accordance to the priorities that God has indicated in the Bible to restore or keep the proper balance in their life's activities. Regarding priorities, Richard Swenson shares how "we love God, spouse, children, self, and church all at the same time, therefore, he suggests the following steps to achieve balance:

1) Regain control over our own lives
2) Place God at the center of all things, and build outward from there
3) Beware the trap of trying to solve the problem of imbalance by becoming even more imbalanced
4) Accept the no given by others[124]

In order to pursue the presence of God and understand His will, non-believer professionals must see these ministry professionals as difference makers who are living a life according to the principles given by God in the Bible.

Follow these practical activities practiced by this author daily to become this type of ministry professional leader:
1. Meditate about who God wants you to be as you are renewed day by day and changed into the image of Jesus Christ.
    a. Pray the Lord's Prayer during the following activities and end each prayer with, "I yield myself to You to do Your will":
        - Wake Up
        - Breakfast
        - Mid-morning

- Lunch
- Mid-afternoon
- Dinner
- Before going to Bed
  b. Follow the Calendar for Daily Reading of Scriptures and "Praying the Psalms" by Elmer L. Towns.
  c. Journalize the presence of God every day.
  d. Pray your prayer list for others every day.
  e. Read one book by a Christian author every three months.
2. Desire to be in the presence of God and live in His power every day.
3. Keep your eyes on eternity not in this temporary earthly life.
4. Look beyond earthly afflictions in view of the eternal glory.
5. Believe God has a purpose to glorify Himself in your life every day.

God has given this author the call to proclaim His name to the professionals in North America metropolises and beyond. Therefore, this work must be carried out with constant prayer "...to God to complete this ministry call He has put within my heart, continually work out the ministry call God has given me and commit to finish by faith the ministry call God has shown me..."[125] Believers need a continuous prayer before God for revival to take place among urban professional in North America and beyond in the way stated by R.A. Torrey:

> It is not necessary that the whole church get to praying to begin with. Great revivals always begin first in the hearts of a few men and women whom God arouses by His Spirit to believe in Him as a living God, as a God who answers prayer, and upon whose heart He lays a burden from which no rest can be found.[126]

Take the time to review the key insights gleaned from this chapter and begin to put them into practice in your own life.

☙ Key Insights from Chapter 5

By not working together with a team mindset with other ministries for the glory of God, many professionals and other evangelized groups have "slipped through the cracks."

The challenge is to evangelize every person in every culture so that he or she believes in Jesus Christ and make them disciples of Christ.

"The real obstacles to becoming fully devoted zealous disciples of Christ are not money, time, methods or knowledge. The major obstacle is the human heart."[127]

There are two rules to consider regarding contentment to relate correctly to money and in similar ways to possessions: 1) God comes first and possessions come second, and 2) possessions are to be used, not loved.[128]

✓ Action Challenges from Chapter 5

"Unless there is ample training for facilitators, a tight accountability process, strong relational connections, and a purposeful selection of material to cover, the small groups will fail to produce disciples."[129]

Go back over the discipleship process advice given by George Barna in his book, *Growing True Disciples* and check off the areas you have already completed in your ministry. Then highlight those areas where your ministry needs to begin to work on.

- ☐ Recognize that disciples making is a process, not a program.
- ☐ The process will not occur without leadership from the senior leadership.
- ☐ The church's ministry focus must be streamline to prioritize and support discipleship.

Practical Implications to Reach Professionals

- ☐ The process is not likely to succeed unless there is a simple but intelligent plan for growth.
- ☐ The process will not generate true disciples unless it has a designated supervisor to facilitate progress, faster creative problem solving and development, and strive for reasonable outcomes.
- ☐ In creating a process that works, adapt lessons learned by other churches to your own ministry context.
- ☐ Be prepared for burnout and complacency to set in after two or three years on involvement in the intensive process.
- ☐ Carefully balance the completion interest of flexibility and structure.
- ☐ Keep your eyes in one goal.[130]

Conclusions
Reaching Professionals

This work has provided the foundation to follow the call by God to reach professionals in metropolises at this time in history.

The ten largest metropolises in North America per the latest census in 2010 are (from largest to smallest):

1) New York, NY
2) Los Angeles, CA
3) Chicago, IL
4) Dallas, TX
5) Houston, TX
6) Philadelphia, PA
7) Washington D.C.
8) Miami, FL
9) Atlanta, GA
10) Boston, MA[131]

Most professionals from the respective state populations live in these cities. These are the areas where the professionals' ministry plans to grow after consolidating the Southeast Florida operation of Miami, Fort Lauderdale, and West Palm Beach. The ministry will be conscious of the current trends in the world and their effects in North American metropolises. These trends include:

- increasing globalization

- the clash of civilizations
- persecution, secularism, postmodernism
- the gap between poor and rich
- the impact of HIV/AIDS
- the growing number of children at risk
- the growing number of refugees
- the number of Christians in non-Western countries, among others.[132]

Furthermore, people cannot ignore the shifts, attitudes, and values they have encountered in our society as we now embrace adequacy against excellence, pessimism against optimism, individual advantage against delayed gratification, inactivity against respect, an amorphous God against a Christian God, skepticism against truth, celebrities against heroes, and experience against knowledge.[133]

Today's perception about churches and ministers by people in metropolises must be taken into consideration since professionals:

➤ Believe church people judge them
➤ Do not want to be lectured
➤ Think church people are a bunch of hypocrites
➤ Do not want religion.

Christians in North American metropolises must not see themselves under the un-biblically based idea of a nice, middle class American Christ by conforming to the following views of their lifestyles:

- He does not mind materialism.
- He would never call them to give away everything they have.
- He does not expect them to forsake their closest relationships so that He receives all of their attention.
- He is fine with nominal devotion that does not infringe on their comforts.
- He wants them to be balanced.
- He wants them to avoid danger altogether.

- He brings comfort and prosperity as they live the American dream.

Part of this study was to research several ministry websites including: John Piper, Marketplace Ministry, City Life Groups, The Other Six Day Ministries, Downtown Bible Study, Capitol Hill Baptist Church, and C12 Group. This author found that none of these ministries focuses upon reaching only professionals, but a more diverse group of the population in North America which includes professionals. A need exists for a ministry focused solely upon effective reaching to professionals in the metropolises of North America.

Both clergy and professionals felt that one-on-one contact is the most effective way to minister to professionals. Personalization is important in business and outreach. As illustrated in other questions included in this research, professionals felt too busy to attend a congregation in which they may just be "another body." By reaching out to professionals on a personal level, ministry members can develop a personal relationship with the professionals, encouraging them in their spiritual growth without the busy professionals feeling pressure to attend a large meeting.

If professionals are not being reached in a way they find effective, they will not respond. Traditional church attendance by professionals has been in steady decline and it would be remiss of ministry members not to change their methods from the comfortable and familiar to a more impactful personal interaction.

The professional's ministry is a ministry to God (worship), believers (nurture), and world (evangelism)[134] in which biblical doctrine, proper use of sacraments, right use of church discipline, genuine worship, effective prayer, witness, fellowship, biblical church government, spiritual power in ministry, personal holiness of life, care for the poor, and love for Christ will be promoted.[135]

To ignite the interest in reaching professionals, a change needs to occur in the way clergy members think about professionals, their priorities, and the reasons they give for not attending church. The ministry challenge is to promote a God-driven environment for professionals to follow the path of biblically based discipleship by the practice of the inward, outward, and corporate disciplines. This ministry aggressively outreaches to professionals with a commitment to cores values like: evangelism, theology, strong pastoral leadership, participatory worship, powerful prayer, centrality of the Holy Spirit, professionals lay ministry, practical Bible teaching, direct missionary involvement, and a low denomination profile.[136]

The reaction to the struggle to reach professionals is to pursue the presence of God by following the urgent call to do His will, live in peace, live in Christ, and live and walk by the Spirit. All of this is to promote the presence of God and know Him in order to develop great energy for God, thoughts for God, contentment in God, and great boldness for God in each of us as individuals first.[137]

This ministry model will work together with the respective metropolitan area's local churches. Appendix A shows prescriptions from churches on how to make a church congregation or ministry healthy.

The ministry methods will follow these general components:

- Leadership team formed by professionals.
- Evangelistic and discipleship gatherings (Sample programs and topics are listed in Appendix B and C.)
- Discipleship gatherings (Sample programs and topics are listed in Appendix D).

The goal is to help professionals to pursue the presence of God by ministering to them when they face life challenges as described in Appendix E, and to encourage them to live a life of simplicity with the suggestions provided in Appendix F. The body of Christ is most effective when it is wholly healthy. By not effectively ministering to a segment of the Christian and world population, we are choosing to let a section of the body of Christ atrophy. Allowing this to happen is contrary to our call as Christians and ministry professionals and negligent given that we have tools at our disposal to reach our brothers and sisters in metropolises.

APPENDIX A
Contemporary Ministry Methods

Here, in outline form and in chronological order, is just a small sampling of prescriptions from various recent authors for the problems of the local church.

Kennon L. Callahan, *Twelve Keys to an Effective Church* (San Francisco: Harper & Row, 1987)
1. specific, concrete missional objectives
2. pastoral/lay visitation in community
3. corporate, dynamic worship
4. significant relational groups
5. strong leadership resources
6. solid, participatory decision making
7. several competent programs and activities
8. open accessibility
9. high visibility
10. adequate parking, land, and landscaping
11. adequate space and facilities
12. solid financial resources

George Barna, *The Frog in the Kettle* (Ventura, Calif.: Regal, 1990)
Ten Critical Achievable Goals…for the 90's (p.226)
1. Win people to Christ
2. Raise Bible knowledge
3. Equip the Christian body

4. Establish Christian community
5. Renew Christian behavior
6. Enhance the image of the local church
7. Champion Christian morals
8. Live by a Christian philosophy of life
9. Restore people's self-esteem
10. Focus on reaching the world for Christ

John MacArthur, *Marks of a Healthy Church* (Chicago: Moody, 1990)
Marks of a Healthy Church (p. 23)
1. godly leaders
2. functional goals and objectives
3. discipleship
4. penetrating the community
5. active church members
6. concern for one another
7. devotion to the family
8. a willingness to change
9. great faith
10. sacrifice
11. worship God

George Barna, *User Friendly Churches* (Ventura Calif.: Regal, 1991)
Ten things successful User-Friendly Churches Don't Do
1. limit God
2. beat a dead horse
3. humiliate visitors
4. insulate themselves from the community
5. alienate those who are different
6. cold-call evangelism
7. apologize for seeking help
8. avoid confrontation
9. base staffing on precedent
10. take the safe route

Bruce Shelley and Marshall Shelley, *The Consumer Church* (Downers Grove, Ill.: Intervarsity, 1992)

Seven vital Steps to Create a Healthy Blend of Effectiveness and Faithfulness (p.226)
1. Identify prevailing values and lifestyles in their ministry context
2. Determine common values with people they would reach
3. Design attractive programs to serve the people they would reach toward
4. View ministries as significant spiritual steps toward the "common life" of the church
5. Be sensitive and receptive to the unchurched
6. "Charm" these seekers into a more mature and explicit expression of Christian discipleship in worship, membership, outreach
7. Reshape the values and lifestyles of new members and enlist them in outreach

George Barna, *Turn-Around Churches* (Ventura Calif.: Regal, 1993)

Eleven Factors of Dying Churches Revived, or Restores to Wholeness (p.42; actually he lists 14)
1. the presence of the Holy Spirit and an openness to His working
2. pastoral love of people; the pastor establishes a bond of trust with the congregation; pastor radically loves his people
3. a new pastor must be brought in to lead a revolution
4. release the past
5. intentionally define types of outreach the church will emphasize
6. equip the laity of effective, targeted ministry
7. pastor must be a strong leader
8. pastor must be hardworking
9. widespread and heartfelt prayer
10. their sermons were a cut or two better than what the congregation had received in the past
11. gaining an objective, outsider's perspective
12. having great staff members
13. having a core of supportive zealots in the congregation
14. long-term pastor

Thom Rainer, *The Book of Church Growth* (Nashville: Broadman & Holman, 1993)
Thirteen Principles of Church Growth (pp.171-316)
1. prayer
2. leadership
3. laity and ministry
4. church planting
5. evangelism
6. worship
7. finding the people
8. receptivity
9. planning and goal setting
10. physical facilities
11. assimilation and reclamation
12. small groups
13. signs and wonders; evident spiritual power

Wayne Grudem, *Systematic Theology* (Grand Rapids, Mich.: Zondervan, 1994)
Twelve signs of a more Pure Church
1. biblical doctrine (or right preaching of the Word)
2. proper use of the sacraments (or ordinances)
3. right use of church discipline
4. genuine worship
5. effective prayer
6. effective witness
7. effective fellowship
8. biblical church government
9. spiritual power in ministry
10. personal holiness of life among members
11. care for the poor
12. love for Christ

Ken Hemphill, *The Antioch Effect: Eight Characteristics of Highly Effective Churches* (Nashville: Broadman & Holman, 1994)
1. supernatural power
2. Christ-exalting worship

3. God-connecting prayer
4. servant leaders
5. kingdom family relationships
6. God-sized vision
7. passion for the lost
8. maturation of believers

Carlyle Fielding Stewart, *African American Church Growth* (Nashville: Abingdon, 1994)
Twelve Principles for Prophetic Ministry
1. celebrate worship
2. invitation in worship
3. informative worship
4. pastor as prophetic clarifier
5. pastor as creative confronter
6. pastor as prophetic restorer and comforter
7. investigative education
8. interpretive education
9. applied education
10. proclamation evangelism
11. propagation evangelism
12. participative evangelism

Thom Rainer, *Giant Awakenings* (Nashville: Broadman & Holman, 1995)
Nine Surprising Trends that Can Benefit Your Church
1. the great prayer movement
2. the rediscovery of the Bible and theology
3. the renewal of the Sunday school
4. the new understanding of culture
5. the new traditional church layperson
6. the new traditional church pastor
7. evangelistic renewal of the traditional church
8. the explosion of church planting
9. the acceptance of multiple worship styles

Rick Warren, *The Purpose Driven Church* (Grand Rapids: Mich.: Zondervan, 1995)
Lots of lists in the book; probably most important are his five purposes, which are also the five components of a purpose statement (pp. 103-107), and his program for church growth (p. 49)
 1. worship: love the Lord with all your heart: church grows stronger
 2. ministry: love your neighbor as yourself: church grows broader
 4. fellowship: baptizing them: church grows warmer
 5. discipleship: teaching them to obey: church grows deeper

Warren advocates that we...
 1. define our purposes
 2. communicate our purposes
 3. organize around our purposes
 4. apply our purposes

C. Peter Wagner, *The Healthy Church, Avoiding and Curing the Nine Diseases that Can Afflict any Church* (Ventura: Calif.: Regal, 1996)
 1. community around the church changes
 2. community the church is in deteriorates
 3. don't understand cultural barriers between us and those we would reach
 4. substituting multi-church evangelism for local church evangelism
 5. being spiritually self-absorbed navel-gazers
 6. inadequate facilities
 7. no spiritual growth
 8. normalism and formalism
 9. the absence of the power of the Holy Spirit

C. Jeff Woods, *Congregational Megatrends*, (Washington, D.C.: Albans Institute, 1996)
Seven megatrends happening in congregations are shifts:
 1. from mass evangelism to relational evangelism
 2. from tribal education to immigration education

3. from surrogate missions to hands-on missions
4. from reasonable spirituality to mysterious spirituality
5. from official leadership to gifted leadership
6. from segmented programming to holographic programming
7. from secondary planning to primary planning

Bill Hull, *Seven Steps to Transform Your Church* (Grand Rapids, Mich.: Revell, 1997)
1. seek renewal
2. develop principled leadership training
3. transform existing leadership
4. cast the vision
5. sacrifice forms for function
6. create community
7. truly do evangelism

Darrell W. Robinson, *Total Church Life* (Nashville: Broadman & Holman, 1997)
Twelve components of Total Church Life Strategy (p. 4)
1. vision
2. commitment
3. leadership
4. unity
5. membership involvement
6. celebrative and joyful worship and praise
7. prayer
8. fellowship
9. organization
10. equipping
11. pastoral care and ministry
12. evangelizing

Mark Shaw, *Ten Great Ideas from Church History* (Downers Grove, Ill.: Intervarsity, 1997)
1. truth (Luther)
2. spirituality (Calvin)
3. unity (Burroughs)

4. assurance (Perkins)
   5. worship (Baxter)
   6. renewal (Edwards)
   7. growth (Wesley)
   8. love for the lost (Carey)
   9. justice (Wilberforce)
  10. fellowship (Bonhoeffer)

James Emery White, *Rethinking the Church* (Grand Rapids, Baker.: 1997; 2nd ed., 2003)
   1. rethinking evangelism
   2. rethinking discipleship
   3. rethinking ministry
   4. rethinking worship
   5. rethinking structure
   6. rethinking community

George Barna, *The Habits of Highly Effective Churches*, (Ventura: Calif.: Regal, 1998)
Highly effective churches:
   1. rely on strategic leadership
   2. are organized to facilitate highly effective ministry
   3. emphasize developing significant relationships within the congregation
   4. invest themselves in genuine worship
   5. engage in strategic evangelism
   6. get their people involved in systematic theological growth
   7. utilize holistic stewardship practices
   8. serve the needy people in their community
   9. equip families to minister to themselves

Brian d. McLaren, *Reinventing Your Church* (Grand Rapids, Mich.: Zondervan, 1998)
Thirteen Strategies
   1. maximize discontinuity
   2. redefine your mission
   3. practice systems thinking

Appendix A

   4. trade up your traditions for tradition
   5. resurrect theology as art and science
   6. design a new apologetic
   7. learn a new rhetoric
   8. abandon structures as they are outgrown
   9. save the leaders
  10. subsume missions in mission
  11. look ahead, farther ahead
  12. enter the postmodern world-understand and engage it
  13. add to this list

Christian A. Schwarz, *The ABC's of Natural Church Development* (Carol Stream, Ill.: Church Smart, 1998)
Eight Quality Characteristics of Growing Churches
   1. empowering leadership
   2. gift-oriented ministry
   3. passionate spirituality
   4. functional structures
   5. inspiring worship service
   6. holistic small groups
   7. need –oriented evangelism
   8. loving relationships

Leith Anderson, "Seven Ways to Rate Your Church" *Leadership* **(Winter, 1999)**
What People Are Looking For
   1. others centered
   2. understanding terminology
   3. people who look like me
   4. healthy problem handling
   5. accessibility

John Bisagno, "Five Characteristics of Successful Churches" *Leadership* **(Unpublished sermon, 1999)**
   1. they all are characterized by strong pastoral leadership
   2. all successful churches are Bible churches, which preach inerrancy and inspiration

3. all successful churches are "good-time churches," emphasizing happiness and celebration
4. all are churches of unity that can't be split
5. all successful churches have an indomitable sense of unrest, an insatiable thirst for more in ministry

Dale E. Galloway, *Making Church Relevant* (Kansas City, Mo.: Beacon Hill, 1999)
Ten Characteristics of a Healthy Churches, Plus One
1. clear-cut vision
2. passion for the lost
3. shared ministry
4. empowered leaders
5. fervent spirituality
6. a flexible and functional structure
7. celebrative worship
8. small groups
9. seeker-friendly evangelism
10. loving relationships
11. evaluation

Stephen Macchia, *Becoming a Healthy Church* (Grand Rapids: Mich.: Baker, 1999)
Ten Characteristics
1. God's empowering presence
2. God-exalting worship
4. spiritual disciplines
5. learning and growing in community
6. servant-leadership development
7. outward focus
8. wise administration and accountability
9. networking with the body of Christ
10. stewardship and generosity

Donald J. MacNair, *The Practices of a Healthy Church* (Phillipsburg: N.J.: Presbyterian & Reformed, 1999)
Three Vital Signs

1. individual members are growing in spiritual maturity
2. the church is actively seeking to help unbelievers come to Christ
3. the absence of major divisions

Six Healthy Practices
1. retain uncompromising commitment to holy Scriptures
2. engage in regular, vibrant worship of God
3. continually train and implement shepherd-leadership
4. mechanism for utilizing gifted member initiative with elder-accountability
5. continually modified vision and plan unique to that church
6. prayerfully seek the grace of God to build commitment to biblical health

Mark Dever, *Nine Marks of a Healthy Church* (Wheaton, Mo.: Crossway, 2000)

1. expositional preaching
2. biblical theology
3. biblical understanding of the good news
4. biblical understanding of conversion
5. biblical understanding of evangelism
6. biblical understanding of church membership
7. biblical understanding of church discipline
8. biblical understanding of church leadership
9. concern for promoting Christian discipleship and growth

Eddie Gibbs, *Church Next* (Downers Grove, Ill.: Intervarsity Press, 2000) (p. 52, citing The Gospel and Our Culture 10, no. 3 [1998])

Twelve Empirical Indicators of a Missional Church
1. proclaims the gospel
2. all members involved are in discipleship
3. Bible is normative
4. church understands itself as different from the world because of its union with Christ
5. seeks to discern God's specific missional vocation for entire community and for all its members

6. behaves Christ-like towards one another
7. practices reconciliation
8. people hold themselves accountable to one another in love
9. practices hospitality
10. worship is central
11. vital public witness
12. recognition that church is an incomplete expression of the reign of God

Herb Miller, "What Priorities Build a Healthy Church?" *The MBA Connection***, Parish Paper (2000)**
Four Main Priorities
1. maturational growth
2. incarnational growth
3. systems growth
4. numerical growth

What Else Counts –Eight More Priorities
1. attitude
2. persistence
3. members who sense that nearby residents are similar to themselves
4. members who strongly emphasize the building of positive relationships with outsiders
5. pastors and staff encouraged that their members understand the main priorities
6. vibrant, sincere prayer
7. numerically declining churches can be strong in incarnational ministries
8. some congregations grow in all four main areas simultaneously

Bob Russell, *When God Builds a Church: Ten Principles for Growing a Dynamic Church* **(West Monroe, La.: Howard 2000)**
1. truth: proclaim God's Word as truth and apply it to people's lives
2. worship: worship God every week in spirit and truth

3. leadership: develop Christ-centered leaders who lead by example
   4. excellence: do your best in every area of service
   5. faith: be willing to step out with a bold faith and take risks
   6. harmony: maintain a spirit of harmony
   7. participation: expect the congregation to participate in every ministry
   8. fellowship: continually practice agape love for one another
   9. stewardship: give generously of God's resources as a church and as individuals
   10. evangelism: commit enthusiastically to evangelism as your primary mission

Report of the Eighteenth Plenary of the Consultation on Church Union (2000)
Nine Visible Marks of Churches Uniting in Christ
   1. mutual recognition of each other as expressions of the one church
   2. mutual recognition of members in one baptism
   3. mutual recognition of ordained ministry
   4. mutual recognition that each affirms the Apostles' and Nicene Creeds
   5. provision for celebration of the Eucharistic together with intentional regularity
   6. engagement together in Christ's mission regularly and intentionally
   7. intentional commitment to promote unity of all persons in church and society
   8. ongoing process of theological dialogue
   9. appropriate structures of accountability and for decision making

Robert Baake, "Ten Leading Indicators of a Healthy Church," *EFCA Beacon* (2001), p. 13
   1. centrality of God's Word
   2. passionate spirituality
   3. fruitful evangelism
   4. high-impact worship

5. mission- and vision-driven
   6. leadership development
   7. church planting
   8. financial stewardship
   9. intentional disciple making
   10. loving relationships

Thom Rainer, "Nine Habits to Attract, Keep Unchurched" *Western Recorder*, **April 17, 2001. p. 10.**
   1. intentionality
   2. cultural awareness
   3. high expectations
   4. clear doctrine
   5. risk taking
   6. dynamic small groups
   7. effective pastoral leadership
   8. effective preaching
   9. prayer

Ed Stetzer, "Prof Lists Ten Commandments for Postmodern U.S. Churches," *Western Recorder*, **February 27, 2001. p. 7.**
   1. be unashamedly spiritual
   2. promote incarnational ministry
   3. worship experientially
   4. preach narrative expository messages
   5. appreciate and participate in ancient patterns
   6. experience visual worship
   7. engage in service
   8. live community
   9. promote team-based leadership

Waldo Werning, *Twelve Pillars of a Healthy Church* **(St. Charles, Ill.: Church Smart, 2001.**
   1. empowering leadership
   2. gift-oriented service/ministry
   3. passionate spirituality
   4. functional structures/administration/servant leadership

Appendix A

---

5. inspiring/high-impact/God-exalting worship services
6. multiplied small groups/intentional disciple making/growing in community
7. witnessing/fruitful evangelism/missions
8. loving relationships
9. centrality of God's Word/Gospel/grace
10. mission- and vision- driven
11. biblical financial stewardship
12. church planting

Andy Stanley and Ed Young, *Can We Do That? Twenty-Four Innovative Practices that Will Change the Way You Do Church* **(West Monroe, La.; Howard, 2002)**

1. Invest and invite: We partner with our regular attenders to reach the unchurched.
2. Targeting the unchurched: We focus on making the unchurched visitor feel welcome and comfortable.
3. Videotaped baptism testimonies: We videotape baptism testimonies and use them as an evangelistic tool during baptismal services.
4. Streaming video: We stream baptisms, dedication services, and sermons on the Internet.
5. Intentional marketing: We are intense about advertising our church to the community.
6. Making membership strategic: We make the membership process a strategic part of emphasizing the small-group, community aspect of church
7. Closing the deal: We hold a Newcomers Class to give information about the church and prepare people to join.
8. Kidstuff: We provide a place where kids take their parents to learn.
9. Aligning student ministry: We understand and plan for the unique relational and ministry needs of junior high and high school students.
10. Welcome teams: We have four distinct teams that focus on specific areas of weekend hospitality.

11. Community groups: We emphasize small groups as a place to find real community.
12. Area fellowships: We utilize Area Fellowships to get people to begin to connect relationally.
13. Group link: We move people from Area Fellowships to Group Link, an environment designed to jump-start small groups.
14. The sports ministry: We have a full-blown athletics ministry without any permanent recreational facilities.
15. Church leadership: We are staff-led church.
16. Ministry team representatives: What? No deacons?
17. Hiring the right people: We hire staff from within the church body.
18. Storytelling: We share ministry stories during staff meetings for inspiration and instruction.
19. Sermon planning: We make the message the first priority of the service and of the pastor.
20. Preaching calendar: We are intentional and deliberate in the timing and topics of our sermon series.
21. Creativity: We creatively adapt the service and the worship center to enhance a creative message.
22. Teaching less for more: We gear our teaching for comprehension and meeting the listeners' needs.
23. Integrating vision: We constantly incorporate the vision of our church into our messages.
24. Personal evaluation: I watch the video of my message every weekend and evaluate my effectiveness.

Gary L. McIntosh, *Biblical Church Growth* (Grand Rapids, Mich.: Baker, 2003)

1. the right premise: God's Word
2. the right priority: glorifying God
3. the right process: discipleship
4. the right power: the Holy Spirit
5. the right pastor: a faithful shepherd
6. the right people: effective ministers
7. the right philosophy: cultural relevance
8. the right plan: target focused

Appendix A

  9. the right procedure: simple structure
10. mix it right

Philip Graham Ryken, *City on a Hill* (Chicago: Moody, 2003)
1. making God's Word plain – expository preaching
2. giving praise to God – corporate worship
3. growing together in groups–fellowship
4. shepherding God's flock – pastoral care
5. thinking and acting biblically–discipleship
6. reaching the world – missions and evangelism
7. serving with compassion – mercy ministry
8. why the church needs the Gospel – repentance and renewal

Peter Scazzero, *The Emotionally Healthy Church* (Grand Rapids, Mich.: Zondervan, 2003)
1. look beneath the surface
2. break the power of the past
3. live in brokenness and vulnerability
4. receive the gift of limits
5. embrace grieving and loss
6. make incarnation your model for loving well

David Garrison, *Church Planting Movements* (Midlothian, Va.: WIG Take Resources 2004)
1. extraordinary prayer
2. abundant evangelism
3. intentional planting of reproducing churches
4. the authority of God's Word
5. local leadership
6. lay leadership
7. house churches
8. churches planting churches
9. rapid reproduction
10. healthy churches

APPENDIX B
Professional Gatherings Program Concept Sample

The following are program samples, one for an evangelistic gathering and the other for a discipleship gathering for the professional's ministry. Actual programs will be developed for the specific approach and methods by the leadership team of the urban professional group.

Evangelistic Gathering:
    Location: Public Setting in a Hotel, Special Club, Ballroom, or Gathering Room
    Day: Tuesday or Thursday
    Time: 6:20 PM – 8:15 PM

Schedule of Activities:
    6:20 PM – 6:30 PM   Welcome and Registration
    6:30 PM – 7:00 PM   Light Dinner and Networking
    7:00 PM – 7:40 PM   Evangelistic Topic

Note. This topic will be presented by using audio visual techniques, panel interview, expository presentation, and others.

    7:40 PM – 8:00 PM   Questions and Answers / Closing Thoughts
    8:00 PM – 8:20 PM   Networking, Ministry Information, and Farewell

Appendix B

Discipleship Gathering:
    <u>Location</u>: Public Setting in a cafeteria or home setting
    <u>Day</u>: Friday
    <u>Time</u>: 6:45 AM – 08:00 AM

Schedule of Activities:
    6:45- 7:00 AM Welcome
    7:00 AM – 7:45 AM Discussion Group around the table while having coffee/breakfast
    7:45 AM – 8:00 AM Closing Thoughts

APPENDIX C
Professionals Gatherings Topics for Evangelism Concept Sample

1. Intelligent Design/Knowing God Concerning Government and Biblical Worldview, The Courts and the Question of Ultimate Power in a Nation, The Protection of Life, Marriage, Family, Economics, The Environment, National Defense, Foreign Policy, Freedom of Speech, Freedom of Religion, Special Groups, Media Bias, Democratic and Republican Policies Today.
2. Evidence of the Resurrection
3. How we got the Bible
4. How to Deal with Anxiety from a Christian Perspective
5. Dealing with Work and Family Pressures
6. The Moral Goodness of Business: Ownership, Productivity, Employment, Commercial Transactions, Profit, Money, Inequality of Possessions, Competition, Borrowing and Lending, Attitudes of Heart, Effects of World Poverty
7. Christian Faith and Atheism: Truth, Divine Design, The First Life, New Life Forms, Jesus and His Resurrection, New Testament Writers, If God Why Evil?
8. Politics According to the Bible: Wrong Views about Christians and Government, Biblical Principles
9. Dealing with Entertainment
10. Dealing with Pornography and Sexual Sin
11. Dealing with the Culture, Society, and Globalization Trends

APPENDIX D
Professionals Gatherings Topics for Discipleship Concept Sample

1. Fundamentals of the Faith: The Bible, God, Jesus Christ, Salvation, Holy Spirit, Prayer, Church, Gifts, God's Will
2. How to Study the Bible: Interpreting the Bible, Reading the Bible, The Cannon of Scripture, The Reliability of Bible Manuscripts, Archeology and the Bible, Languages Testaments
3. Christian Character: Faith, Humbleness, Forgiveness, Self-Discipline, Hope, Worshipping God
4. Christian History Timeline
5. The Lord's Prayer
6. The Armor of God
7. Making Sense of the Bible: The Word of God, The Canon of Scripture, Scripture Authority, Clarity Necessity and Sufficiency, The Inerrancy of Scripture
8. Making Sense of Who God Is: Existence of Know-ability, Character, Trinity, Creation, Providence, Miracles, Prayer, Angels, Satan, and Demons
9. Making Sense of Men and Sin: The Creation Man, The Essential Nature of Man, Sin, The Covenants Between God and Man
10. Making Sense of Christ and the Spirit: The Person of Christ, The Atonement, Resurrection and Ascension, The Offices of Christ, The Work of the Holy Spirit

11. Making Sense of Salvation: Common Grace, The Gospel, Regeneration, Conversion, Justification, Adaption, Sanctification
12. Making Sense of the Future: The Return of Christ, The Millennium, The Final Judgment, The New Heavens and New Earth

APPENDIX E
Practical Experiences from the Life of Professionals

Following are some experiences I have known from the life of professionals who live in North America metropolises. They show how some professionals have a hard time communicating with other professional believers. This author does not intend to judge the people in the stories, but to draw practical implications related with the particular experience in the light of this study. Following are short versions of these experiences in which general conditions, observations, and practical implications related to the circumstances are described. This researcher knows these people personally and had conservations at length with the professionals involved in the stories due to his longevity and relationship over three decades as a professional, and having worked with them in other companies.

Professional A/Experience 1 – Working for a professional who professed being a believer.

General Conditions: **Professional A** worked for this company for over a decade. He found the owner, who professed to be a born again Christian, to be all about making money with a practical approach and mentality. This attitude was expressed in his complete lack of witness of Christ as seen by his Christian employees, who felt this owner saw them as instruments given by God to him to achieve material wealth. This individual never showed sensitivity to the needs of **Professional A** though the owner was sensitive to an incompetent professional of his own ethnic group.

Observations: This owner and his company are no longer in business. He is remembered by many who know him, as a "good" professional, but one who did not build a legacy or care for his employees except when they were making money for him.

Practical Implications: I had the opportunity to know this owner in my professional and church networking activities. He never mentioned in our conversions his Christian worldview and gave me the impression that the only thing that mattered in his conversation with other professionals was the business and its profit side. I attended his retirement party fifteen years ago, where he shared about his plans of traveling, but nothing about Christ.

Professional B/Experience 2 – Doing business with other professional and non-professional believers.

General Conditions: **Professional B**'s company was hired to provide consulting services to a company whose owner was a self-made non-professional professing Christ millionaire. **Professional B**'s company was hired because his group's quality control review of a project designed showed major inefficiencies that caused the owner of a third believer-run organization to ask the self-made non-professional millionaire company to reconsider their design work.

Observation: The relationship between **Professional B's** company and self-made non-professional professing Christ millionaire appeared to be going very well. Suddenly, **Professional B** received an email firing him. **Professional B** made several attempts to contact the self-made non-professional millionaire by phone and seemingly resolved the issue to be a misunderstanding. **Professional B** took it upon himself to visit this company's headquarters to further reconcile differences and was met with minimum cooperation and interaction in regard to the project. Days after that trip, out of nowhere attacks were leveled against **Professional B's** integrity, making unfounded accusations against in regard to their consulting work.

Practical Implications: **Professional B** was open about his faith in Christ since the two other companies involved professed to be Christian organizations. The self-made non-professional professing

Christ millionaire accused **Professional B** of openly talking about Christ in front of his company's non-believing professionals. **Professional B** has evidence against the false accusations and continues to deal in an ethically way with this situation.

Professional C/Experience 3 – Working for a believer supervisor.
General Conditions: **Professional C** was hired by company where a professing born again Christian was his immediate supervisor. This supervisor was not tolerant about anything related with Christianity while at work. He did not allow prayer to take place during employee meals, even though all the people attending the event were in acceptance of prayer. **Professional C** was reprimanded by this supervisor regarding the prayer request.

Observations: The supervisor appeared to have an attitude towards **Professional C** after that. However, to his credit, when the supervisor left the company he apologized to **Professional C** for the way he treated him during the four years they worked together.

Practical Implications: The supervisor then acknowledged his wrongdoing to the supervisor. Without the negative attitude from the supervisor toward **Professional C**, they could have given the other employees in the company a witness of two believers working together in the pursuit of God's will. Unfortunately, this was not the case.

Professional D/Experience 4 – Professional providing consulting services to a church congregation.
General Condition: **Professional D** provided design services for a congregation building in which they hired an out of town builder. This builder wanted to short out on the cost of the construction for his maximum profit and, therefore, provide the congregation with lesser quality materials and systems from what was designed. **Professional D** made this known to the congregation's senior pastor who took no action. The church building was built. **Professional D** later found out that the builder made enough profit to retire while the pastor ran away with a woman other than his wife.

Practical Implications: This example shows, among other lessons, what appears to be a selfish personal goal approach to serving in ministry.

Professional E/Experience 5 – Professional helping a church congregation with consulting services for a new worship center building.
General Conditions: **Professional E,** a believer, assisted a church congregation and their architect with consulting services without getting paid for the services rendered. The church leadership made a verbal commitment that the project would be designed by **Professional E's** company and his non-believer architect. Over the next year, they invested their time to attend meetings and provided design work to the church in order to assist them with their project budget.
Observations: **Professional E** worked diligently in order to satisfy the church leadership demands and encourage the non-believing professional architect to go along with the project due to the fact they were dealing with believers who would do the right thing. However, the church congregation went with a design/build team with no regards to all the work done by **Professional E** and his architect team.
Practical Implications: This experience shows the lack of this church's consideration to the time and work by others, believers and non-believers. It was not a good witness to any of those involved.

APPENDIX F
A Call to Simplicity by Professionals from the book by Richard A. Swenson, MD, Margin

The following are suggestions that will assist in simple living. Beware of the distinction between suggestions and rules, for if you make them rules, you will have converted simplicity into legalism and defeated its purpose before even beginning.

Possessions and Finances
- Cultivate contentment, desire less.
- Resist covetousness.
- Resist consumerism.
- Wage war against advertisements.
- Buy things for their usefulness rather than their status.
- De-accumulate.
- Develop the habit of giving away.
- Share possessions.
- Offer the use of your possessions – don't make others ask.
- Develop a network of exchange.
- Avoid overindulging – for example, toys, food, movie viewing, etc.
- Avoid impulse buying.
- Don't buy now, pay later.
- Avoid credit cards if they are problem.

- Reject fashion, especially fads.
- De-emphasize respectability
- Simplify your wardrobe – give away excess.
- Learn how to make do with a lower income instead of needing a higher one.

Pace and Atmosphere
- Slow down.
- Do not exhaust your emotional bank account.
- Lie fallow.
- Say no.
- Enjoy peaceful music.
- Control/restrict/eliminate television watching; surfing the net.
- Get a remote control and turn off advertisements.

Relationships
- Cultivate a closeness with God.
- Schedule "simple" dates with your spouse.
- Teach your children
- Enjoy family field trips.
- Practice regular hospitality.
- Help each other, emphasize service.
- Encourage others.
- "Always speak the truth and you'll never be concerned with your memory."
- Don't judge.
- Learn to enjoy solitude.
- Have wise counsel from your spouse and godly colleagues.

Appreciation
- Send cards of encouragement and appreciation when others are not expecting it.
- Be grateful for things large and small.
- Emphasize a joyful life.
- Appreciate creation.

Spiritual Life
- Make Christ and the Scriptures central.
- Meditate, memorize.
- Pray.
- Encourage simple worship.

Activities
- Make your commitments simple.
- Don't overwork.
- Fast periodically from media, food, people.
- Elevate reading, go to the library.
- Simplify Christmas.
- Write down those things you need to remember and forget everything else.

Nutrition and Exercise
- Exercise.
- Bike or walk.
- Make your recreation active rather than passive.
- Develop healthy sleep habits.
- Avoid overeating.
- Frequent a co-op.
- Whenever possible, buy food directly from those who grow it.
- Garden

APPENDIX G
A Practical Implementation of Reaching and Equipping Professional in a Local Church

(*This is an active church which has a program of equipping and ministering to professionals. So it serves as an example of how one church actively engages and equips professionals.*)

Hill Country Bible Church (HCBC) in Austin, Texas, provides weekly Sunday school classes, quarterly seminars, conferences and weekly Bible studies, leadership and discipleship classes, and weekly small group meetings in members' homes to equip adult and student believers for sharing the gospel and starting spiritual conversations with their co-workers, friends, and neighbors. HCBC provides curriculum resources at the meetings and classes as well as online resources, like videos and PDF outlines, when you miss a meeting. Just a few of these training resources include:

1. **exploreGod** (http://www.exploregod.com/): A Web site which provides credible content (videos, articles, blogs) to help people answer their spiritual questions. Believers are encouraged to meet socially with neighbors and co-workers to discuss questions like:
    a. Does life have a purpose?
    b. Is there a God?

c. Why does God allow pain and suffering?
   d. Is Christianity too narrow?
   e. Is Jesus really God?
   f. Is the Bible reliable?
   g. Can I know God personally?
2. **The Art of Neighboring**: Twenty-one churches in Denver challenged people in their congregations to be intentional in relationships with neighbors on their street. (www.artofneighboring.com)
3. **The Great Adventure** at HCBC: **backyard Bible clubs** and summer festival in the church parking lot. Brings thousands of kids to neighborhood houses to hear the gospel. Then they bring their parents to the summer festival on the final night. www.hcbc.com/ministries/great-adventure/

HCBC provides practical ways to reach neighbors and co-workers with the gospel by engaging with co-workers, their families and community as the hands and feet of Christ to meet their physical and emotional as well as spiritual needs. These outreach programs include:

1. **Christian financial management classes**. Great resources for co-workers and their adult children who are having financial management problems.
   a. Financial Peace University: biblically-based curriculum for churches, plus used in 25% of public high schools. Teaches people, including students, how to handle their money God's way. Developed by Dave Ramsey and his team of experts. (www.daveramsey.com/fpu/)
   b. Crown Financial Ministries: equips people to live by God's design for their finances, work, and life. (www.crown.org)
2. **Celebrate Recovery** small group meetings at churches to deal with all of life's hurts, habits, and hang-ups. Similar to Alcoholics Anonymous but has stronger Biblical basis and addresses broader range of issues. Originally launched 20 years ago by Saddleback Church (where Rick Warren is the pastor). (www.celebraterecovery.com)

3. **DivorceCare** weekly seminars to help parents and kids work through divorce-related issues (anger, self-esteem, boundaries) in an atmosphere of hope and support. (www.hcbc.com/find-help/divorcecare/)
4. **GriefShare** small groups to help people deal with the loss of a family member or friend. (www.hcbc.com/find-help/griefshare/)
5. **Faith in Action – Drive a Senior.** Church and community volunteers drive seniors to the doctor, grocery, senior center, beauty shop, or help around their house. Great resource to refer to co-workers who are caregivers for their parents. Volunteers are encouraged to engage in spiritual conversations with the seniors they drive. (www.driveasenior.org)
6. **Poverty and health-related drives** for food, clothes, backpacks, blood, Christmas gifts. Easy to engage co-workers in giving to these drives, and can lead to spiritual conversations. Use company giving campaigns and online community volunteer databases to engage co-workers. Example: IBM On Demand Community (www-01.ibm.com/ibm/ondemand-community/home/index.jsp)
7. **Recruit school volunteers** for reading literacy, mentoring, father-figures (WATCH D.O.G.S.), prayer (Mothers in Prayer), scouts, and free school feeding programs. HCBC has online recruiting to engage church and corporate volunteers through the Chamber of Commerce and using corporate online recruiting (like IBM). (www.fathers.com/watchdogs/) (www.mothersinprayer.org)
8. **English as a Second Language (ESL) classes**. Churches and other community organizations offer ESL classes to help people who are non-native English speakers improve their English and learn American culture. Spouses of professional international employees are interested in ESL classes. Young college graduate missionaries go to foreign countries to teach native English in the universities in East Asia and South America.
9. **Teaching trades and skills**, such as electrical trade skills, car mechanics, computer hardware/software, community

gardens. Invite co-workers to volunteer to teach their skills at church and community-based job training resource centers. Christian professionals can share their faith with other professionals in non-work settings. (www.hcbc.com/serve/community/economic-development/) (www.rivercityhope.org)

10. **Job Seekers Network** offers help on resumes, interview skills, LinkedIn, networking techniques, financial management, and career direction from Christian coaches experienced in corporate, educational, non-profit, and other industries. 100+ job seekers attend every week, from all faiths, and hear the gospel. (www.jobseekersnetwork.org)

11. **Austin Disaster Relief Network** is comprised of churches, ministries and businesses within the Austin Christian community to form a disaster relief alliance to help those in need during disasters, both in Austin and elsewhere. Another way to involve corporate professionals as volunteers working alongside Christians. (www.adrntx.org)[138]

APPENDIX H
Some Website Resources

Some Websites of Leaders offering equipping and resources for ministry involving Christian professionals:

Campus Crusade (http://www.campuscrusade.com/PA/workplacekit.htm)

Dean Niewolny (www.halftime.org)

Dr. Buddy Crum (http://www.marketplacealliance.com/)

Ed Silvoso (www.edsilvoso.com)

John Maxwell (www.johnmaxwell.com)

Os Hillman (www.marketplaceleaders.org)

The Navigators (http://www.metronavs.org/workplace)

Tim Keller (www.redeemer.org)

APPENDIX I
A Prayer for the Professionals Ministry

Our Awesome Holy, Holy, Holy God Who created us, I thank You for creating me for a life in Your service and to work on this Ministry in order to reach professionals in North American metropolises and beyond.

You deserve all our worship and our surrendered lives. Please let this Ministry work proclaim You are Holy, Holy, Holy around the World. You Who are in heaven are omnipotent, omniscience, omnipresent. May Your Holy, Holy, name be given all worship by all people touched by the work of this Ministry.

May Your kingdom be manifested in our lives, rule in our hearts, and be manifested in our actions as You lead this Ministry through the lives of believers who are controlled by Your Holy Spirit. May Your sovereign will be done so You are glorified in our lives on Earth and in the Heavenly places.

Let this Ministry be a testimony of Your glory and mighty power as all of us who are part of it follow Your will in all areas of our lives. Provide for all our physical needs from food, shelter, job, education, health, and relationships as we carry on the command to make disciples in North American metropolises and beyond.

You, our God, receive all glory and honor in all areas of our lives and the urban

Professional Ministry in North America metropolises. Let us forgive all who do wrong to us as You have forgiven us and given us

Your unconditional love. As we go through this life and Ministry pilgrimage on this Earth and face temptation may we be victorious.

Deliver us from evil as we fight the spiritual warfare to proclaim your Holy, Holy, Holy

Name to all the people of the World in our lives and this Ministry work. You and You alone are the Kingdom, and the power and glory forever and ever. Amen

Bibliography

Barna, George. *Futurecast: What Today's Trends Mean for Tomorrow's World*. Austin, TX: Tyndale House Publishers, 2011.

Barna, George. *Maximum Faith: Live Like Jesus*. Austin, TX: Fedd and Company, 2011.

Barna, George. *Growing True Disciples: New Strategies for Producing Genuine Followers of Christ*. Colorado Springs, CO: WaterBrook Press, 2001.

Baxter, Richard, and J. M. Houston. *Watch Your Walk: A Pattern for Personal Growth and Ministry*. Colorado Springs, CO: Victor Books, 2005.

Bickers, Dennis. *The Bivocational Pastor: Two Jobs, One Ministry*. Kansas City, MO: Beacon Hill Press of Kansas City, 2004.

Blackaby, Henry, Claude King, and Richard Blackaby. *Fresh Encounter: God's Plan for Your Spiritual Awakening*. Nashville, TN: B&H Books, 2009.

Blackaby, Henry T. and Avery T. Willis Jr. *On Mission with God*. Nashville, TN: B&H Publishing Group, 2002.

Bonar, Horatious. *Words to Winners of Souls*. Phillipsburg, NJ: P & R Publishing, 1995.

Bridges, Jerry. *Growing Your Faith*. Colorado Springs, CO: Navpress, 2004.

Bridges, Jerry. *Trusting God*. Colorado Springs, CO: Navpress, 2008.

Chambers, Oswald. *If You Will Ask*. Grand Rapids, MI: Discovery House Publishers, 1994.

Cho, David Yonggi. *Prayer That Brings Revival*. Lake Mary, FL: Charisma House, 1998.

Clowney, Edmund P. *Called to the Ministry*. Phillipsburg, PA: P & R Publishing, 1976.

Coleman, Robert E. *Master Plan of Discipleship, The*. Grand Rapids, MI: Revell, 1998.

Coleman, Robert E. *The Master Plan of Evangelism with Study Guide*. Grand Rapids, MI: Revell, 1993.

Crabb, Dr. Larry. *Connecting: Healing Ourselves and Our Relationships*. Nashville, TN: Thomas Nelson, 2005.

Crabb, Dr. Larry. *Real Church: Does It Exist? Can I Find It?* Nashville, TN: Thomas Nelson Publications, 2006.

Cymbala, Jim. *Breakthrough Prayer: The Power of Connecting with the Heart of God*. Grand Rapids, MI: Zondervan, 2003.

Cymbala, Jim, with Stephen Sorenson. *The Church God Blesses*. Grand Rapids, MI: Zondervan, 2002.

Dallimore, Arnold A. *George Whitefield: God's Anointed Servant in the Great Revival of the Eighteenth Century*. Reprint ed. Wheaton, IL: Crossway Books, 2010.

Dever, Mark. *9 Marks of a Healthy Church*. Wheaton, IL: Crossway Books, 2004.

Edwards, Jonathan. *Praying Together For True Revival*. Phillipsburg, N.J: P & R Publishing, 2004.

Falwell, Jerry. *Building Dynamic Faith*. Nashville, TN: Thomas Nelson, 2007.

Bibliography

Falwell, Jonathan. *Innovative Church: Innovative Leadership of the Next Generation in Church.* Nashville, TN: B & H Publishing Group, 2008.

Finney, Charles. *How to Experience Revival.* New Kensington, PA: Whitaker House, 2010.

Finney, Charles G. *Holy Spirit Revivals: How You Can Experience the Joy of Living in God's Power.* New Kensington, PA: Whitaker House, 1999.

Foster, Richard. *Celebration of Discipline.* London, England: Hodder & Stoughton, 1998.

Gazelka, Paul. *Market Place Ministries.* Lake Mary, FL: Creation House Press, 2003.

Geisler, Norman L. *Inerrancy.* Grand Rapids, MI: Zondervan, 1980.

Geisler, Norman L and Frank Turek. *I Don't Have Enough Faith to be an Atheist.* Wheaton, IL: Crossway Books, 2004.

Grudem, Wayne. *Systematic Theology: An Introduction to Biblical Doctrine.* Grand Rapids, MI: Zondervan, 1994.

Grudem, Wayne. *Making Sense of the Church.* Grand Rapids, MI: Zondervan, 2011.

Guthrie, Stan. *Missions in the Third Millennium: 21 Key Trends for the 21st Century.* Colorado Springs, CO: Paternoster, 2002.

Harton, David, *The Portable Seminary.* Grand Rapids, MI: Bethany House Publisher, 2006.

Hansen, Collin, and John Woodbridge. *A God-Sized Vision: Revival Stories That Stretch and* Stir. Grand Rapids, MI: Zondervan, 2010.

Lahaye, Jerry B. Jenkins, Tim. *Are We Living in the End Times?* Carol Stream, IL: Tyndale House Publishers, 1984.

Lawrence, Brother. *The Practice of the Presence of God.* Shippensburg, PA: Destiny Image, 2007.

Lutzer, Erwin. *Conquering the Fear of Failure*. Ann Arbor, MI: Vine Books, 2002.

MacArthur, John. *Alone with God*. Wheaton, IL: Chariot Victor Publishing, 1995.

MacArthur, John. *Ashamed of the Gospel: When the Church Becomes Like the World*. 3rd ed. Wheaton, IL: Crossway Books, 2010.

MacArthur, John. *The Truth War: Fighting for Certainty in an Age of Deception*. Nashville, TN: Thomas Nelson, 2008.

MacDonald, James. *Gripped by the Greatness of God*. Chicago, IL: Moody Publishers, 2005.

Malphurs, Aubrey. *A New Kind of Church: Understanding Models of Ministry for the 21st Century*. Grand Rapids, MI: Baker Books, 2007.

Malphurs, Aubrey. *Planting Growing Churches For the 21st Century: A Comprehensive Guide For New Churches and Those Desiring Renewal*. 3rd ed. Grand Rapids, MI: Baker Books, 2004.

McDowell, Josh. *The New Evidence That Demands a Verdict*. [Rev., updated, and expanded]. ed. Nashville, TN: Thomas Nelson, 1999.

McNeal, Reggie. *The Present Future: Six Tough Questions for the Church (Jossey-Bass Leadership Network Series)*. San Francisco, CA: Jossey-Bass, 2009.

McIntosh, Gary L. *Taking Your Church to the Next Level: What Got You Here Won't Get You There*. Grand Rapids, MI: Baker Books, 2009.

Noll, Mark A. *A History of Christianity in the United States and Canada*. Grand Rapids, MI: William B. Eerdmans Publishing Company, 1992.

Olson, David. *The American Church in Crisis* Grand Rapids, MI: Zondervan, 2006.

Ortberg, John. *The Life You've Always Wanted: Spiritual Disciplines for Ordinary People*. Grand Rapids, MI: Zondervan, 2009.

Bibliography

Ortberg, John. *The Me I Want to Be: Becoming God's Best Version of You*. Har/Psc ed. Grand Rapids, MI: Zondervan, 2009.

Packer, J. I. *Knowing God*. Dawners Grove, IL: Intervarsity Press, 1973.

Packer, J. I. *Faithfulness and Holiness (Including the Full Text of the First Edition of Ryle's Classic Book, Holiness / Redesign): The Witness of J. C. Ryle*. Reprint ed. Wheaton, IL: Crossway Books, 2010.

Packer, J.I. *Keep in Step with the Spirit: Finding Fullness in Our Walk with God*. Rev. and enl. ed. Grand Rapids, MI: Baker Books, 2005.

Palau, Luis. *Changed by Faith: Dare to Trust God with Your Broken Pieces... and Watch What Happens*. Carol Stream, IL: Tyndale House Publishers, Inc., 2011.

Payne, Ruby. *Framework for Understanding Poverty*. Highlands, TX: aha! Process, 1996.

Piper, John. *Brothers, We Are Not Professionals: A Plea to Pastors For Radical Ministry*. Nashville, TN.: B & H Books, 2002.

Piper, John. *Desiring God, Revised Edition: Meditations of a Christian Hedonist*. Rev Exp ed. Colorado Springs, CO: Multnomah Books, 2011.

Piper, John. *Don't Waste Your Life*. Wheaton, IL; Crossway Books, 2003.

Piper, John. *Let the Nations Be Glad!* Grand Rapids, MI.: Baker Academic, 2003.

Piper, John. *The Hidden Smile of God (Paperback Edition): The Fruit of Affliction in the Lives of John Bunyan, William Cowper, and David Brainerd (Swans Are Not Silent)*. Wheaton, IL: Crossway Books, 2008.

Piper, John. *Rethinking Retirement: Finishing Life for the Glory of Christ*. Bklt ed. Wheaton, IL: Crossway Books, 2009.

Platt, David. *Radical: Taking back your faith From the American Dream*. Colorado Springs; CO. Multnomah Books: 2011.

Polhill, John. *The New American Commentary Volume 26 Acts*. Nashville, TN: Broadman Press, 1992.

Reeves, Gary L. McIntosh...R. Daniel. *Thriving Churches in the Twenty-First Century: 10 Life-Giving Systems for Vibrant Churches*. Grand Rapids, MI: Kregel Academic & Professional, 2006.

Riss, Richard M. *Survey of 20th-Century Revival Movements in North America, A*. Peabody, MA: Baker Academic, 1988.

Rizzo, Dino. *Servolution: Starting a Church Revolution through Serving*. Grand Rapids, MI: Zondervan, 2009.

Sage, Bob. *Envy: The Enemy Within*. Ventura, CA: Regal, 2003.

Sanders, J. Oswald. *Spiritual Leadership: Principles of Excellence for Every Believer*. Chicago, IL: Moody Publishers, 2007.

Saucy, Robert L. *The Church in God's Program (Handbook of Bible Doctrine)*. Wheaton, IL: Moody Publishers, 1972.

Scazzero, Peter. *Emotionally Healthy Church, The*. Grand Rapids, MI: Zondervan, 2003.

Schaeffer, Francis A. *The Church at the End of the Twentieth Century*. 2 ed. Wheaton, IL: Crossway Books, 1985.

Schreiner, Thomas R., and Bruce A. Ware, eds. *Still Sovereign: Contemporary Perspectives On Election, Foreknowledge & Grace*. Grand Rapids, MI.: Baker Academic, 2000.

Stanley, Dr. Charles F. *How to Listen to God*. Nashville, TN.: Thomas Nelson, 2002.

Stott, John. *Sermon On the Mount (Lifeguide Bible Studies)*. Student/Stdy Gde ed. Downers Grove, IL: IVP Connect, 2000.

Stowell, Joseph M. *Shepherding the Church: Effective Spiritual Leadership in a Changing Culture*. Chicago, IL: Moody Publishers, 1997.

Streett, R. Alan. *The Effective Invitation: A Practical Guide for the Pastor.* Updated ed. Grand Rapids, MI: Kregel Academic & Professional, 2004.

Swenson, Richard. *March: Restoring Emotional, Physical, Financial, and Time Reverses to Overloaded Lives,* Colorado Springs, CO: NavPress, 2004.

Swindoll, Charles R. *The Church Awakening: An Urgent Call for Renewal.* New York, NY: Faith Words, 2010.

Taylor, J. Hudson. *Hudson Taylor (Men of Faith).* 2 ed. Minneapolis, MN: Bethany House, 1987.

Taylor, Howard. *Spiritual Secret of Hudson Taylor.* New Kensington, PA.: Whitaker House, 2011.

Thomas, Curtis C. *Practical Wisdom for Pastors: Words of Encouragement and Counsel for a Lifetime of Ministry.* Wheaton, IL: Crossway Books, 2001.

Torrey, R. A. *How to Pray.* Seattle, WA: Create Space, 2011.

Towns, Elmer L. *365 Ways To Know God.* Downers Grove, Illinois: Regal, 2004.

Towns, Elmer. *Big Bold Extraordinary Faith Work Text.* Class notes unpublished Spring, 2009.

Towns, Elmer L. *God Encounters: To Touch God and Be Touched by Him.* Ventura, CA: Regal Books, 2000.

Towns, Elmer. *How God Answers Prayer (How to Pray).* Shippensburg, PA: Destiny Image, 2009.

Towns, Elmer L. *Praying the Lord's Prayer for Spiritual Breakthrough.* Ventura, CA, U.S.A.: Regal, 1997.

Towns, Elmer. *Revival and Church Growth Work Text.* Boston: Harcourt and Brace, n.d.

Towns, Elmer. *Spiritual Factors of Church Growth Work Text*. (unpublished, n.d.), 14.

Towns, Elmer L. *What's Right with the Church: A Manifesto of Hope*. Ventura, CA: Regal, 2009.

Tony, Felicity Dale, and George Barna. *The Rabbit & the Elephant: Why Small Is the New Big For Today's Church*. Carol Stream, IL: Barna Books, 2009.

Walvood, John and Ray Zuck. *The Bible Knowledge Commentary New Testament*. Colorado Springs, CO: Victor, 2004/

Warren, Rick. *The Purpose Driven Life (QR Code Enhanced Edition): What On Earth Am I Here For? (Purpose Driven Life, The)*. Pap/Psc En ed. Grand Rapids, MI: Zondervan.

White, Peter. *The Effective Pastor. The Key Things a Minister Must Learn to Be*. Bemidji, MN: Mentor / Christian Focus, 2011.

Willmington, Harold L. *The Outline Bible*. Wheaton, IL: Tyndale House Publishers, Inc., 2000. 2011.

Wubbels, Lance, ed. *Hudson Taylor on Spiritual Secrets (30-Day Devotional Treasuries)*. Austin, TX: Emerald Books, 2002.

Glossary

believer. Those who by grace and through faith in the atoning work of Christ have been regenerated by the Holy Spirit. However, in common usage it often includes those who claim an evangelical conversion experience.
carousing. Drink alcohol, and enjoy oneself with others in a noisy, lively way
Christian. Any who professes to be a follower of Christ. The term embraces all traditions and confessions of Christianity. It is no indicator of the degree of commitment of theological orthodoxy.
church. Any assembly, local bodies of Christian believers, or the universal body of all believers.
church planting. The starting of churches is termed church planting.
dispute. A disagreement or argument.
dissension. Disagreement that leads to discord.
drunkenness. Drunk, especially habitually.
envy. Discontented or resentful longing aroused by another's possessions, qualities, or luck.
evangelism. Active calling of people to respond to the message of grace and commit oneself to God in Jesus Christ.
fasting. Deliberate and generally prolonged abstention from eating (and sometimes drinking) as a means of humbling oneself before God.
fellowship. The communion or common faith experiences and expressions shared by the family of believers, as well as the intimate relationship they have with God.
function. An activity that is natural to or the purpose of a person or thing.

gospel. Good news, specifically the good news of salvation through Jesus Christ.

Great Commission. The final series of commands of the Lord Jesus Christ before His Ascension for His followers to evangelize, baptize, disciple, and teach all the people of the world.

idolatry. Any ultimate confidence in something other than God.

immorality. Sexual activity contrary to biblical principles.

impurity. The quality or condition of being impure.

jealousy. Envious of someone else's possessions, achievements, or advantages.

kingdom of God. Concept of God's kingly or sovereign rule, encompassing both the realm over which rule is exerted and the exercise of authority to reign.

local church. A local fellowship of believers. The word is commonly used to mean a church building or church service, but here this usage has largely been avoided.

meditation. Act of calling to mind some supposition, pondering upon it, and correlating it to own life.

metropolis. A very large and busy city.

missionary. One who is sent with a message. This word of Latin derivation has the same basic meaning as the wider use of the term "apostle" in the New Testament. The Christian missionary is one commissioned by a local church to evangelize, plant churches, and disciple people often on a foreign mission field away from his home area and often among people of a different race, culture or language.

outburst of anger. A strong feeling of annoyance, displeasure, or hostility.

people group. A significantly large sociological grouping of individuals who perceive themselves to have a common affinity with one another. From the viewpoint of evangelization, this is the largest possible group within which the gospel can be spread without encountering barriers of understanding of acceptance.

prayer. Any form of communication with God on the part of believing people in response to situations that may arise in life.

professional. A person having impressive competence in a particular activity.

renewal. A quickening or enlivening in personal commitment to Christ in the churches, Charismatic renewal in the historic denominations is an example.

revival. the restoring to life of believers and churches which have previously experienced the regenerating power of the Holy Spirit but have become cold, worldly and ineffective. Often wrongly used of evangelistic campaigns, revival really signifies a sovereign act of God as an answer to prayer in bringing about a religious awakening and outpouring of the Spirit on His people.

sensuality. Relating to the physical senses, especially as a source of pleasure.

solo. An isolated approach to team work and collaboration.

sorcery. The attempted manipulation of events through charms, amulets, incantations, and the like.

strife. Angry or bitter disagreement; conflict.

study. The devotion of time and attention to acquiring knowledge, especially from books.

urban. Relating to a town or city.

Western World. The countries of Europe, North America, and Australasia.

About the Author

Doctor Ralph Baeza is a professional consulting engineer, and church minister and pastor, in the Southeastern Florida region in North America. He has worked in different Church Congregation positions and ministries during the past forty years and as a career professional engineer for over three decades. Doctor Baeza completed his Doctor of Ministry program with concentration in Evangelism and Church Growth at Liberty Baptist Theological Seminary. His thesis work focused in Church Ministries to reach urban professionals in North America metropolises and beyond.

Doctor Baeza holds the following academic degrees: Doctor of Ministry (Evangelism and Church Growth), 2013 Liberty Baptist Theological Seminary, Lynchburg, Virginia; Master of Divinity (Church Ministries), 2008 Liberty Baptist Theological Seminary, Lynchburg, Virginia; Master of Arts (Religion), 2006 Trinity Evangelical Divinity School, Deerfield, Illinois; Master of Business Administration, 1991 National Autonomous University of Honduras, Tegucigalpa, Honduras, this degree has been verified as comparable to those by U.S. accredited universities; Bachelor of Science in Electrical Engineering and Bachelor of Science in Industrial Engineering, 1984 National Autonomous University of Honduras, Tegucigalpa, Honduras. These degrees have been verified as comparable to those by U.S. accredited universities. Doctor Baeza is currently pursuing the Doctor of Business Administration with concentration in Organizational Leadership in the School of Business at Liberty University, Lynchburg, Virginia.

Doctor Baeza was born and raised in Madrid, Spain and has lived in the United States of America since 1986 with his wife Alice and children, Mary Elizabeth, Leodanny (Mary's husband), Georgette, Benjamin (Georgette's husband), Natalie and Daniel (Natalie's husband).

The following verse from the Holy Scriptures, the Bible, summarizes Pastor Baeza's purpose in this life for the glory and honor of his Holy, Holy, Holy God:

For from Him and through Him and to Him are all things. To Him be the glory forever. Amen. (Romans 11:36)

Endnotes

1. Steve Green, Partial Lyrics from The Song, *"The Mission."*
2. John Piper, *Let the Nations be Glad* (Grand Rapids, MI: Baker Academic, 2003), 160.
3. Other books that use biblical foundational principles and introduce innovative methods in which to reach the new and changing world view are: *Innovate Church, 11 Innovations in the local Church, The Shaping of Things to Come, Taking your Church to the next level, How to Multiply your Church,* and *A New Kind of Church. Growing True Disciples, The Pillars of Christian Character, Maximum Faith, The Practice of the Presence of God, Knowing God, The Pursuit of Holiness, Growing Your Faith, Trusting God.*
4. Larry Crabb, *Real Church: Does It Exist? Can I Find It?* (Nashville, TN: Thomas Nelson Publications, 2009), 147.
5. John Piper, *Let the Nations Be Glad* (Grand Rapids. MI: Baker Academic, 2003), 43.
6. David Horton, *The Portable Seminar* (Grand Rapids. MI: Baker Publishing Group, 2006), 548.
7. ⁶ Ibid., 549.
8. Ibid., 550-561.
9. Stan Guthrie, *Missions in the Third Millennium* (Colorado Springs, CO: Paternoster, 2002), 249.
10. Robert E. Coleman, *The Master Plan of Discipleship* (Grand Rapids, MI: Revell, 1998), 10, 11.
11. Robert Coleman, *The Master Plan of Discipleship* (Gran Rapids, MI: Revell, 1998), 121.

12 Horatius Bonar, *Words to Winners of Souls* (Boston, MA: P&R Publishings, 1995), 59.
13 Rudy Payne, *A Framework Understandings of Poverty* (Highlands, TX: aha! Process, Inc., 1996), 42.
14 Ibid., 43.
15 David Horton, *The Portable Seminary* (Grand Rapids, MI: Baker Publishing Group, 2006), 576.
16 Ibid., 577-581.
17 George Barna, *Futurecast* (Austin, TX: Tyndale House Publishers, Inc., 2011), IX.
18 Ibid., X.
19 Ibid., 60.
20 Ibid., 79
21 Thom Schultz, *Why People Don't Want to go to Church Anymore* (March 3, 2012)
22 Ibid.
23 George Barna, *What People Experience in Churches*, January 9, 2012
24 Ibid.
25 David Olson, *The Church in Crisis* (Grand Rapids, MI: Zondervan, 2008), 28.
26 Ibid., 37.
27 David Platt, *Radical* (Colorado Springs, CO: Multnomah Books, 2011), 13.
28 Stan Guthrie, *Missions in the Third Millennium* (Colorado Springs, CO: Paternoster, 2002), 23.
29 Henry Blackaby and Henry Willis, *On Mission with God* (Nashville, TN: B&H Publishing Group, 2009), 3.
30 James McDonald, *Gripped by the Greatness of God* (Chicago, IL: Moody Publishers, 2009), 133.
31 Ibid., 162.
32 Ibid., 163.
33 Richard Riss, *A Survey of 20th Century Revival Movements in North America* (Peabody, MA: Baker Academic, 1988), 7.
34 John MacArthur, *The Truth War* (Nashville, TN: Thomas Nelson, 2008), 9.
35 Ibid., 10-11.

36 Ibid., 12.
37 Ibid., 28-32.
38 Ibid., 215.
39 Norman Geisler and Frank Turek, *I Don't Have Enough Faith to be an Atheist* (Wheaton, IL: Crossway Books, 2004), 20.
40 Ibid., 24.
41 Ibid., 28.
42 Norman Geisler, *Inerrancy* (Grand Rapids, MI: Zondervan, 1980), 294.
43 Ibid., 295-304.
44 John MacArthur, *Ashamed of the Gospel* (Wheaton, IL: Crossway Books, 2010), 26.
45 Ibid., 26.
46 Ibid., 42.
47 Ibid., 63.
48 Ibid., 76.
49 Ibid., 76.
50 Ibid., 78.
51 http://www.facebook.com/pages/marketplace-ministries-of.../112291572185642
52 Ibid.
53 Paul Gazelka, *Marketplace Ministers* (Lake Mary, FL: Creation House Press, 2003), 146.
54 http://www.citylifechurch.com/lifegroups/
55 http://www.theother6days.com
56 http://www.downtownbible.org
57 http://www.capitolhillbaptist.org
58 http://www.c12group.com
59 Aubrey Malphurs, *A New Kind of Church* (Grand Rapids, MI: Baker Books, 2007), 42.
60 Wayne Grudem, *Making Sense of the Church* (Grand Rapids, MI: Zondervan, 2011), 34.
61 Elmer Towns, *Perimeter of Light* (Ventura, CA: Revell, 2004), 22.
62 Ibid. 22.
63 Wayne Grudem, *Making Sense of the Church* (Grand Rapids, MI: Zondervan, 2003), 54.

64 Ibid. 55.
65 Jonathan Falwell, *Innovative Church* (Nashville, TN: B & H Publishing Group, 2008), 106-107.
66 Elmer Towns, *What is Right with the Church* (Ventura, CA: Regal, 2009), 24.
67 Jonathan Falwell, *Innovate Church* (Nashville, TN: B&H Publishing Group, 2008), 112.
68 Elmer Towns, *Perimeters of Light* (Wheaton, IL: Moody Publishers, 2004), 33.
69 Wayne Grudem, *Making Sense of the Church* (Grand Rapids, MI: Zondervan, 1994), 136.
70 Robert Coleman, *The Master Way of Personal Evangelism* (Grand Rapids, MI: Revell, 1993), 11.
71 Ibid., 141-158.
72 George Barna, *Growing True Disciples* (Colorado Springs, CO: WaterBrook Press, 2001), 2.
73 Ibid. 23.
74 Ibid. 27-28.
75 Richard Foster, *Celebration of Discipline* (London, GB: Hodder & Stoughton, 1998), 1.
76 Ibid., 1
77 Ibid., 13, 76
78 Ibid., 77, 140
79 Ibid., 141, 201
80 Elmer Towns, *11 Innovations in the Local Church* (Ventura, CA: Regal, 2009), 74.
81 Aubrey Malphurs, *A New Kind of Church* (Ventura, CA: Regal, 2007), 24.
82 Ibid. 35.
83 Ibid. 50.
84 Ibid. 51-52.
85 Elmer Towns, *Worktext Spiritual Factors of Church Growth* (unpublished, n.d.), 7.
86 J I Packer, *Knowing God* (Downers Grove, IL: Intervarsity Press, 1973), 24-32.
87 Ibid. 32.
88 Ibid. 40.

89 Brother Lawrence, *The Practice of the Presence of God* (Alachua, FL: Bridge-Logos, 1999), 13.
90 John McArthur, *The Pillars of Christian Character* (Ventura, CA: Regal, 2009), 12.
91 Jerry Bridges, *The Pursuit of Holiness* (Ventura, CA: Regal, 2009), 29-30.
92 Elmer Towns, *Perimeters of Light* (Chicago, IL: Moody Publishers, 2004), 17.
93 Ibid., 191.
94 Gary McIntosh, *Taking your Church to the Next Level* (Grand Rapids, MI: Baker Books, 2009), 198-203.
95 Peter Scazzero, *The Emotionally Healthy Church* (Grand Rapids, MI: Zondervan, 2003), 118-119.
96 Elmer Towns, *Perimeters of Light* (Chicago, IL: Moody Publishers, 2004), 64-65.
97 John Polhill, *The New American Commentary Volume 26 Acts* (Nashville, TN: Broadman Press, 1992), 487.
98 Ibid., 498.
99 Ibid., 492-510.
100 Elmer Towns, *Perimeters of Light* (Chicago, IL: Moody Publishers, 2004), 173.
101 Ibid., 179-180.
102 George Barna, *Growing True Disciples* (Colorado Springs, CO: WaterBrook Press, 2001), 167-168.
103 Ibid., 167-168.
104 John Polhill, *The New American Commentary Volume 26 Acts* (Nashville, TN: Broadman Press, 1992), 378.
105 Elmer Towns, *Revival and Church Growth Work Text* (Boston: Harcourt and Brace), 6.
106 Ibid., 164-165.
107 Larry Crabb, *Real Church* (Nashville, TN: Thomas Nelson, 2009), 153.
108 Charles Swindoll, *The Church Awakening* (New York, NY: Faith Words 2010), 27.
109 George Barna, *Growing True Disciples* (Colorado Springs, CO: Waterbrook Press, 2001), 121.
110 Ibid., 127-132.

111 John Piper, *Desiring God* (Sisters, OR: Multnomah Publishers, 2003), 321.
112 Jerry Bridges, *Trusting God* (Colorado Springs, CO: NavPress, 1999), 9.
113 Jerry Bridges, *Growing Your Faith* (Colorado Springs, CO: Multnomah Publishers, 2004), 37.
114 Ibid., 120.
115 Ibid., 131.
116 Ibid., 167.
117 Ibid., 177.
118 George Barna, *Maximum Faith* (Austin, TX: Fedd and Company, Inc., 2011), 17-24.
119 Elmer Towns, *Big Bold Extraordinary Faith Work Text* (Spring, 2009), 141.
120 Ibid., 235.
121 Richard Swenson, *Margin* (Colorado Springs, CO: NavPress, 2004), 33.
122 Ibid., 164.
123 Ibid., 188.
124 Ibid., 190.
125 Jerry Falwell, *Building Dynamic Faith* (Nashville, TN: World Publishing, 2005), 21.
126 R. A. Torrey, *How to Pray* (Chicago, IL: Moody Publishers, 2007), 121.
127 Ibid., 167-168.
128 Ibid., 164.
129 George Barna, *Growing True Disciples* (Colorado Springs, CO: Waterbrook Press, 2001), 121.
130 Ibid., 127-132.
131 http://www.quickfacts.census.gov/gfd/states
132 David Horton, *The Portable Seminary* (Grand Rapids, MI: Baker Publishing Group, 2006), 571-581.
133 George Barna, *Futurecast*. (Austin, TX: Tyndale House Publishers, Inc, 2011), 7
134 Wayne Grudem, *Making Sense of the Church* (Grand Rapids, MI: Zondervan, 2011), 46-51.
135 Ibid., 54.

136 Elmer Towns, *Spiritual Factors of Church Growth* (unpublished, n.d.), 7
137 J. I. Packer, *Knowing God* (Downers Grove, IL: Intervarsity Press, 1973) 24 – 32.
138 Compiled by Cathy Laws, member of HCBC.

Printed in the USA
CPSIA information can be obtained
at www.ICGtesting.com
LVHW011226030823
753912LV00009B/245